The New Zealand Herald
Guide to
Auckland

PENGUIN BOOKS

PENGUIN BOOKS

Published by the Penguin Group

Penguin Books (NZ) Ltd, cnr Airborne and Rosedale Roads, Albany,
Auckland 1310, New Zealand

Penguin Books Ltd, 80 Strand, London, WC2R ORL, England

Penguin Group (USA) Inc., 375 Hudson Street, New York, NY 10014,
United States

Penguin Books Australia Ltd, 250 Camberwell Road, Camberwell,
Victoria 3124, Australia

Penguin Books Canada Ltd, 10 Alcorn Avenue, Toronto,
Ontario, Canada M4V 3B2

Penguin Books (South Africa) (Pty) Ltd, 24 Sturdee Avenue, Rosebank,
Johannesburg 2196, South Africa

Penguin Books India (P) Ltd, 11, Community Centre, Panchsheel Park,
New Delhi 110 017, India

Penguin Books Ltd, Registered Offices: 80 Strand, London, WC2R ORL, England

The New Zealand Herald, a division of APN New Zealand.
PO Box 32, 46 Albert St, Auckland, New Zealand.
Ph: (64 9) 379 5050 Fax (64 9) 373 6420
Website: www.nzherald.co.nz

First published by Penguin Books (NZ) Ltd and The New Zealand Herald, 2003

1 3 5 7 9 10 8 6 4 2

Designed by Mary Egan
Typeset by Egan-Reid Ltd
Printed in Australia by McPherson's Printing Group

ISBN 0-14-301886-8

www.penguin.co.nz

Contents

Maps

Introduction

Auckland is a city alive with local culture. From an urban scene to rival any vibrant international city to the lure of its many beaches, islands in the gulf, multicultural festivals, native bush walks, the great Maori and Pacific collections of the famous Auckland museum or internationally renowned vineyard tours – Auckland's got it all.

Whatever your lifestyle, this guidebook contains information of interest to you.

The *New Zealand Herald Guide to Auckland* is accessible and subjective, with lively opinions about a cross-section of the many activities and attractions in Auckland. An annual publication, this guide is the *New Zealand Herald*'s view of what makes Auckland a great and multi-dimensional city.

This book would not have been possible without the contribution of many of the *Herald*'s fine journalists, writers and photographers, the organisational skills of Lauri Tapsell and the generous support of the editor-in-chief Gavin Ellis.

Every attempt has been made to ensure all information is accurate and up-to-date at the time of printing. However, because Auckland is a constantly changing city, we recommend that you check details of places and events via the contact information given to avoid any potential disappointments.

We hope you will find this handy pocket guide a useful reference. If you have any comments about it, please let us know.

The Publishers, Penguin Books (NZ) Ltd,
Private Bag 102902, NSMC, Auckland, or email: aucklandguide@penguin.co.nz

EMERGENCY PHONE NUMBERS

Check the front section of the Auckland Telephone Book for other emergency phone numbers and information not listed here.

Police, Ambulance, Fire   Ph: 111
From a mobile phone   Dial: '111' and then 'Call' or 'Send'

Accident and Emergency Clinics/ Public Hospitals

Auckland Central

Auckland Hospital, Park Rd, Grafton   Ph: 379 7440
Starship Children's Hospital, Park Rd, Grafton   Ph: 307 4949

South Auckland

Middlemore Hospital, Hospital Rd, Otahuhu   Ph: 276 0000

North Shore

North Shore Hospital, Shakespeare Rd, Takapuna   Ph: 486 8900

For private accident and medical centres and emergency doctors throughout the city, refer to the Auckland Telephone Book under 'Registered Medical Practitioners and Medical Centres' in the front section.

Seven-days-a-week Emergency Dentists

Try the hospitals, or call:

Auckland Dental Group, 134 Remuera Rd, Remuera   Ph: 520 6609
Ponsonby A&E Dental Unit, 202 Ponsonby Rd, Ponsonby   Ph: 376 9222

NON-EMERGENCY PHONE NUMBERS

Police Central City Station, Vincent St   Ph: 302 6400
Fire Central City Station, Pitt St   Ph: 302 5412
Ambulance Central City Station, Pitt St   Ph: 579 9099
Traffic report problems (From mobile)   Ph: *555

OTHER USEFUL PHONE NUMBERS

Auckland Airport flight information   Ph: 256 8899

Transport

Buses, trains, harbour ferries information   Ph: 366 6400

Taxis

Auckland Co-op Taxis	Ph: 300 3000
Alert Taxis	Ph: 309 2000

Tourism Auckland Information Centre

Sky City, Atrium, Auckland Central	Ph: 363 6000
Amex Viaduct Harbour, Waterfront	Ph: 979 2333

Healthcare for Travellers (vaccination, medical checks)

TravelCare, Level 5, Dingwall Building,
87 Queen St, Auckland Central   Ph: 373 4621

Travellers Health Centre Worldwide,
72 Remuera Rd, Newmarket   Ph: 520 5830

Auckland City Council city information   Ph: 379 2020
Auckland Regional Council   Ph: 366 2000 /
                                              0800 80 60 40

    Parks   Ph: 303 1530
    Environment   Ph: 366 2070

Finding Your Feet

Auckland Facts & Figures

POPULATION

The greater metropolitan area of Auckland, New Zealand's largest city, is home to 1.1 million people, around one-third of the country's population. The Auckland urban area (2001 Census: from Waiwera in the north to Drury in the south) lays claim to being the world's largest Polynesian city.

PEOPLE

The 2001 Census recorded the ethnicity of Aucklanders as being (in round figures):

> 68 percent European ethnic origin,
> 12 percent Maori (compared with 15 percent in the whole of New Zealand),
> 14 percent Pacific Islanders (6.5 percent in the whole of New Zealand), and
> 14 percent Asian (6.6 percent in the whole of New Zealand).

NB: The total for Auckland is greater than 100 percent because of people claiming links with more than one ethnic group.

The average age of Aucklanders is 33 years, with a quarter of the population aged under 15.

HIGH-RANKING CITY

Auckland is ranked fifth equal – alongside Sydney, Frankfurt,

Copenhagen and Bern – in the annual quality-of-life survey of 215 cities by Mercer Human Resource Consulting. Rankings are based on 39 criteria including: political, social, economic and environmental factors; personal safety and health; education; transport and other public services.

In terms of cost of living, Mercer Human Resource Consulting ranked Auckland 115th out of 144 cities worldwide, where the most expensive place to live, at number 1, was Tokyo and Moscow.

INCOME

The median income of Aucklanders is $21,200 compared with $18,500 for the whole of New Zealand. Nearly 50 percent of Aucklanders aged 15 and over have an annual income of less than $20,000 (15 percent earn more than $50,000 annually). The Census found unemployment in the Auckland urban area was 8 percent (7.5 percent for all of New Zealand).

LANGUAGE

The Census lists the most common language in the Auckland urban area after English as Samoan, spoken by 5.3 percent of the city's population. More than 70 percent of urban Aucklanders speak only one language.

GEOGRAPHY

Situated between two harbours, the Waitemata and Manukau, the city is built on plenty of hills, more than 50 of them being volcanic cones (extinct, we are told) which are thousands of years old. The circular-shaped volcano of Rangitoto is visible in the harbour from all parts of the city.

CLIMATE

Auckland's temperate coastal climate is without extremes.

Legend has it that a few snowflakes fell in the bush surrounds of suburban Titirangi in 1951.
Bright sunshine hours: 2021 per annum.
Average annual rainfall: 1301 mm.

TEMPERATURE

Summer average: maximum around 24° C (75 F), minimum around 16° C (61 F).
Winter average: maximum around 15° C (59 F), minimum around 8° C (46 F).

SEASONS

Summer: Dec to Feb
Autumn (Fall): Mar to May
Winter: Jun to Aug
Spring: Sept to Nov

BUSINESS AND SHOP HOURS

Business and office hours are usually 8.30 am–5 pm Mon to Fri; shops, standard opening hours are 9 am–5 pm Mon to Fri, 10 am–4 pm Saturday & Sunday. Shopping malls open 7 days and often have longer opening hours. Some late-night shopping is available on Thursday or Friday nights (until 9 pm). Bank opening hours are 9 am–4.30 pm Mon to Fri. A few banks are also open on Saturdays.

2004 PUBLIC HOLIDAYS

New Year's Day	1 January
Day after New Year's Day	2 January
Auckland Anniversary Day	26 January
Waitangi Day	6 February
Good Friday	9 April
Easter Monday	12 April
ANZAC Day	25 April
Queen's Birthday	7 June
Labour Day	25 October

| Christmas Day | 25 December |
| Boxing Day | 26 December |

DRIVING

Most rental car companies will ask for an International Driver's Licence and drivers must be over 21. The most important traffic rule to remember: when turning left, give way to all traffic turning into the same street from the right.

Drink Driving

It is illegal to drive while under the influence of alcohol. Police carry out random breath-testing and you may be asked to take a blood test. If you are involved in a car accident, police are also likely to require a blood test. Depending on the circumstances, penalties could range from fines, loss or disqualification of your licence, to imprisonment. The legal limit is 80 mg of alcohol per 100 ml of blood. Though effects of alcohol vary from person to person it is generally considered safe for men drivers to drink two and a half cans of beer in the first hour, half a can per hour after that; and for women drivers, one and a half glasses of wine in the first hour, and one-third of a glass per hour following.

Safety Belts

These must be worn. It is the driver's responsibility to make sure all passengers under the age of 15 are buckled in. You could be fined $150 for each belt not worn. Anyone over 15 years is personally responsible for ensuring they are wearing a seat belt.

Road Rules

New Zealanders drive on the left side of the road. The maximum speed limit in a built up area – towns and cities – is 50 kmph. On highways and motorways it is 100 kmph.

GOODS & SERVICES TAX

New Zealand has a 12.5 percent goods and services tax,

known as GST. Retailers are encouraged to make all prices inclusive of GST, but be wary of some sellers and restaurants that state a price, which then has to be calculated 'plus GST'.

POSTAL SERVICES

Post shops exist inside other shops, as well as on their own. Look for their red, white and black colouring and the NZ Post logo (an envelope symbol). Booklets of stamps are available at supermarket checkouts, stationery shops, dairies and convenience stores. Post boxes can be found on various streets.

PUBLIC TELEPHONES

Public telephones activated by phone cards or coins are located all over the city. Phone cards are available from supermarkets, dairies, convenience stores, service stations and other outlets. New Zealand's International Access Code is 64, and the area code for Auckland is 09 (drop the 0 if phoning New Zealand from overseas).

SUNBURN

New Zealand's clear, unpolluted atmosphere and low latitudes produce sunlight that is stronger than much of Europe or North America, so wear a hat and sunscreen if you plan to be out in the sun for more than 15–20 minutes.

DAYLIGHT SAVING

Daylight Saving begins on the first Sunday in October and finishes on the third Sunday in March. (Clocks move forward one hour during this period.) New Zealand is close to the International Date Line and is 12 hours ahead of Greenwich Mean Time.

TIPPING AND SERVICE CHARGES

Tipping is not compulsory in New Zealand but those in service industries (restaurants, hotels) appreciate being tipped for good service.

LEGAL AGES

You must be 15 years of age to:

> Drive a vehicle on public roads (as long as you hold at least a learner's driving licence).

You must be 18 years of age to:

> Stand for and vote in Parliament or local body elections,
> Buy alcohol in a pub or from a shop,
> Place a bet at the TAB or races,
> Buy cigarettes.

You must be 20 years of age to:

> Bet in a casino.

DRUGS

Those found in possession of Class B drugs such as cannabis oil, morphine and opium, could face a prison sentence of up to three months or face a fine of $500. The manufacturing, importing or supplying of Class B drugs could result in a prison sentence of up to 14 years. Methamphetamine, or speed (and 'pure' methamphetamine or 'P') is set to be reclassified as a Class A drug in 2004. Police have the power to search for a Class A drug without a warrant if they suspect it is being made, dealt or used. The maximum sentence for manufacturing, importing or supplying Class A drugs, including heroin, LSD and cocaine, is life imprisonment.

PROSTITUTION

Law reform in 2003 decriminalised the sex industry. This allows brothels and massage parlours to operate their businesses within health and safety standards and local body bylaws.

SMOKING

The lighting up of cigarettes, cigars or pipes is prohibited in most public places. This includes theatres, shops, shopping malls, on public transport and in nearly all workplaces. A bill before Parliament to ban smoking in bars, pubs and restaurants is likely to become law in April 2004.

Tuning In

If you want to tune in while in Auckland, there should be something to suit your taste in the many radio and television programmes available around the metropolitan area.

RADIO STATIONS
IN ORDER OF FREQUENCY

FM

Mai FM	88.6	Hip-hop, rap and dance music, Maori and youth
Newstalk ZB	89.4	Talkback, sport, news, current affairs, nostalgia
The Rock	90.2	Loud rock, blokey attitudes
91ZM	91.0	Middle-of-the-road music
More FM	91.8	Middle-of-the-road music
Concert FM	92.6	Classical music
Solid Gold	93.4	Hits from the 50s, 60s and 70s
The Edge	94.2	Top 40 music
95bFM	95.0	University student radio, alternative music
Cool Blue	96.1	Jazz & blues
George FM	96.8	Dance music/ electronica
Classic Hits 97FM	97.4	Hits from the 70s, 80s, 90s and today
i98FM	98.2	Easy listening
Hauraki 99FM	99.0	Classic rock
Life FM	99.8	Christian radio
National Radio	101.4	Public radio, news, current affairs, traditional music, cultural/arts focus
Planet FM	104.6	Multilingual/community

AM

531 PI	531	Pacific Island channel
Pacific	702	Talkback, horse-racing commentary
National Radio	756	Public radio, news, current affairs, traditional music, cultural/arts focus
Southern Star	882	Christian music
BBC Chinese Service	990	Mandarin and Cantonese, London, local programmes
Newstalk ZB	1080	Talkback, sport, news, current affairs, nostalgia
Ruia Mai	1179	Maori programmes
Rhema	1251	Christian programmes
Radio Sport	1332	Sports news, talkback, commentaries
BBC World Service	1476	International feed from London
Radio Samoa	1593	Samoan music, news

TELEVISION CHANNELS

TV ONE	News, current affairs, drama, sport, documentaries.
TV 2	Youth viewing, drama, soaps, movies.
TV 3	News, movies, sport, documentaries.
C4	Youth-oriented music video channel.
PRIME	Australian current affairs, lifestyle, drama, movies.
TRIANGLE	Local community programmes.
SKY TELEVISION	Pay-TV service featuring sports, news, movies, music, children's programmes, lifestyle, documentaries. Pay-per-view is also an option.

Getting Around

Aucklanders are known for their love affair with cars, which have traditionally been the easiest (if not the only) way to get around the urban sprawl fast. They have fallen into the trap, of course, of spending frustrated hours on the congested motorways which – to be honest – could be your worst experience of Auckland. Navigating Auckland by public transport is the alternative. The network of buses, ferries and trains have most of the city covered, and the new Britomart Transport Centre provides a central connection point for these services. A golden rule: the further you want to travel, the more planning will be required. This guide to commuter services will get you moving around the city and provides for some DIY sightseeing tours.

GETTING STARTED

Tourism Auckland Visitor Information Centre,
Ph: 979 2333 for all visitor enquiries.

Website: www.aucklandnz.com

Advice, transport timetables and tourist information are available from Auckland Visitor Centre locations:

i-SITE Auckland
Atrium, SKYCITY Auckland, cnr Victoria and Federal Sts.
Open: Sun to Wed, 8am–8pm, Thurs to Sat, 8am–10pm

New Zealand Visitor Centre
AMEX Viaduct Harbour, cnr Quay and Hobson Sts, Downtown Auckland.
Open: 7 days, 9am–6pm (Labour Weekend (Oct) – Easter); rest of year
9am–5pm

Auckland International Airport Information Centre
Arrivals Lounge, Auckland International Airport.
Open: 7 days for all arriving international flights

Auckland Domestic Airport Information Centre
Air New Zealand Terminal, Auckland Domestic Airport.
Open: 7 days, 7am–5pm

**Rideline, Toll free Ph: 0800 10 30 80 if you are in the Auckland region.
If outside the free calling area Ph: 09 366 6400.**

Website: www.rideline.co.nz

This is a free information service for buses, trains, and ferries throughout the Auckland region. Rideline answer questions over the phone and will mail out any timetables on request, even putting together a package specifically for your needs. The website allows you to compile itineraries etc, as well as gather info on fares and timetables.

Open: Mon to Sat, 7 am–8 pm, Sun & public holidays, 8 am–6.30 pm. Closed Christmas Day.

CATCHING BUSES

Auckland has about 500 different bus routes, connecting the inner city to the edges of the Auckland region. Buses are by far the cheapest way to see the city, for locals and visitors. You can pretty much get to (or at least get close to) anywhere, but some parts of the city are better serviced than others.

As a general rule, services run Monday to Saturday from 6 am–11 pm, and on Sundays and public holidays from 8 am–10 pm.

Fares depend on how far you go, but they start off from 50 cents within the inner city and range to about $9 for the longest trips. There are concessions for pre-paid multiple tickets, and for children under 16, senior citizens and students. An Auckland Discovery Day Pass ($12 per adult) allows you to travel around most of the region on buses, trains and ferries for a day.

TIPS: Signal to the driver with a wave as the bus approaches. Have the correct fare available, or use pre-paid Smartcards.

Where to go by bus

The majority of buses depart from Britomart Transport Centre, Victoria St or Wellesley St.

To see Auckland for $1.20: The Link (City Loop)

The Link bus service is a fast and simple way to get a feel for inner Auckland's layout.

Link buses run every 10 minutes Monday to Friday 6am–7pm, every 15 minutes every evening to 11.30pm, every 10 minutes on Saturday 7am–6pm and every 15 minutes on Sunday 7am–11.30pm The distinctive white Link buses run in both directions on a loop route from Customs St East and take in the Britomart Transport Centre, Parnell, Newmarket, Auckland Hospital, Auckland University, Karangahape Rd, Ponsonby and Victoria Park Markets.

Link bus stops are marked with a blue and white sign. The fare? Just $1.20 to anywhere on the route.

Free 'City Circuit' Bus

There is a free service that runs clockwise in a loop around key destinations such as The Edge entertainment area, Auckland University, the Viaduct Basin and Queen St. Bright red timetable cases are situated at all stops, and the buses dedicated to this route are also bright red in colour to help distinguish them from other services.

Buses also run up and down Queen St every five minutes weekdays, and every 10 minutes on week nights and week-ends. Look for routes 015–045 on the bus destination sign.

Getting Across Town

The Urban Express service, route 006, offers a 30-minute ride between shopping centres at St Luke's Mall and

Newmarket. It runs Monday to Friday between 6 am–10.30 pm. These buses can also be hailed from the roadside at certain times.

Other cross-town routes include the 008 (from Manukau City Centre and Otahuhu to Onehunga and New Lynn) and the 009 (from Panmure to Onehunga and New Lynn).

FERRIES

Being a city of two harbours, Auckland's waterways are part playground, part highway. Ferries are becoming increasingly important to commuters, especially as a link to Auckland's North Shore. The city is most beautiful seen from the water.

Many of the Hauraki Gulf's scenic islands can also be reached by boat, and in addition to the commuter services listed here, there are many tours and charters available if you want to spend a day on the harbour. See Island-Hopping, page 49.

Travelling by ferry is not cheap, though daily travellers say the peacefulness makes up for it. The cost is not prohibitive if you want to make a day out of sightseeing. Most ferries leave from the ferry terminal on the downtown waterfront.

Fullers (Ph: 367 9111, Website: www.fullers.co.nz) operate most of the commuter services, which are listed by destination here:

Devonport:
Daily and frequent services. Costs (return fare): adults $8, children $4. Connects with buses to Takapuna, Cheltenham, Narrow Neck, Stanley Bay and Bayswater.

Stanley Bay (naval dockyards):
Mon to Fri, peak times only. Costs (return fare): adults $8, children $4.

Bayswater:
Daily sailings, less frequent on weekends and public holidays, and excluding Christmas Day. Connects with buses to Takapuna, Wairau Park, Auckland City, AUT Akoranga Campus, Milford and Devonport. Costs (return fare): adults $8, children $4.

Birkenhead:
Daily sailings, less frequent on weekends and public holidays, and excluding Christmas Day. Birkenhead wharf is within walking distance of the Highbury shops, where you can catch buses to Beachhaven and Takapuna, or two buses to reach Link Drive in Wairau Park (via Glenfield). Costs (return fare): adults $8, children $4.

Half Moon Bay:
Daily sailings, less frequent on weekends. Does not operate on public holidays. Costs (return fare): adults $13, children $7.

Rangitoto Island:
Departs daily (including public holidays) from Auckland via Devonport. The trip takes approximately 30 minutes. Costs (ferry only): adults $20, children $10; (ferry plus guided tour): adults $49, children $25.

Waiheke Island:
Daily sailings (including public holidays) connect with Waiheke bus services. For the Waiheke vehicle ferry information, see below. Costs (return fare): adults $24, children $12.

Great Barrier Island:
Service runs Labour Weekend (Oct) – Easter. See timetable on www.fullers.co.nz/timetables/gbarrier or Ph: 367 9111. The trip takes approximately two hours. Bookings essential. Costs (return fare): adults $118, children $56, family $298.

Waiheke Island Vehicle Ferry:

Subritzky Shipping Line (Ph: 534 5663, Website: www.subritzky.co.nz) operates a drive-on vehicular ferry between Half Moon Bay and Kennedy Pt on Waiheke. The service runs 7 days a week. Advance bookings essential.

TIPS: Get to the wharf early. If the weather is really bad ring the ferry company to check if service is operating, especially for ferries to the islands.

TRAINS

Tranz Metro (Ph: Rideline 366 6400) commuter trains run Mon to Sat between the central city and Waitakere City in the west, and between Auckland Central and Papakura in the south (there are two variations of the southern route). There is no Sunday service.

Trains leave the city from the Britomart Transport Centre. The fare depends on how far you want to go, starting from $1.10 for adults and 70 cents for a child for one stage. Various passes and concessions are available.

TIPS: Get to the station early and have the correct change ready.

TAXIS AND SHUTTLES

The best way to find a taxi is on the rank (go to the car at the front of the rank) or by phoning in an order (under 'Taxis' in the telephone directory Yellow Pages). Two of the biggest firms are Co-op Taxis on Ph: 300 3000 and Alert Taxis on Ph: 309 2000. Both will quote prices over the phone.

For door-to-door shuttle services to the airport, start with SuperShuttle, Ph: 0800 74 88 85 or look under 'Shuttle' in the Yellow Pages.

By day, the Air Bus leaves from the city every 20 minutes for the airport (and vice versa), stopping in at most major hotels and backpackers in Auckland city. Air Bus operates

365 days a year. Tickets are available from the driver, Ph: 0508 AIRBUS (0508 247 287) or Ph: 375 4702 for more information. Website: www.airbus.co.nz

RENTAL CARS

Avis, Budget, Hertz are available, all with outlets in the city and at the airport. There are many other companies too. Look under 'Rental cars' in the Yellow Pages to find the most convenient outlet or to shop around for the best deal.

Hertz	Ph: 0800 654 321
Budget	Ph: 0800 652 227
Avis	Ph: 526 2847

Recreation

10 Top Views

From several of the top vantage points in Auckland, you can witness the panorama of a city with two harbours which lead off into different oceans, the Pacific in the east and the Tasman Sea in the west. The isthmus separating the two masses of water is only 2 km wide at its narrowest point (at Otahuhu). There was a time, when electric trams ran, that Auckland had the only coast-to-coast tramway in the world, from the bottom of Queen Street in the city to Onehunga.

Upper Harbour from the Sky Tower

Rangitoto from North Head.

City from the Devonport Ferry.

From up high, you can see images of the city as colour – green (massive tree plantings, parks, the volcanic cones, the Waitakere Ranges), red (corrugated iron and tile roofs), white (the predominant house colour). The New Zealand tradition of a house on its own piece of land is evident. The suburban sprawl stretches as far as the eye can see, even as multi-storeyed apartment blocks proliferate, principally in the central business district. The open access to water everywhere around the Auckland region contributes to the spacious vista.

FROM MT EDEN

Mt Eden Rd, Mt Eden.
Open to people and vehicles 24 hours a day. Free entry.
The cone of this volcano is 196 m high, and the bowl-shaped crater from which the volcano exploded is 50 m deep. Apart from the local views, a direction table indicates where over the horizon major cities of the world are to be found. Sample distances are pinpointed by arrows. The direction table, presented in 1928 by city philanthropist and later mayor Sir Ernest Davis, was originally of Royal Doulton porcelain. It was destroyed by vandals in 1988 and the present bronze replacement installed.

Cows wander the slopes, but not the summit where sensitive archaeological evidence of early Maori occupation (kumara pits, terraces) is still visible.

FROM ONE TREE HILL

Entrances from Manukau Rd, Royal Oak; Greenlane Rd West, Greenlane; and Campbell Rd, Onehunga.
Open to people 24 hours a day, vehicles 7 am to dusk. Free entry.
Drive or walk through the 200-plus ha reserve, Cornwall Park, to the summit of One Tree Hill (or Maungakiekie: 'maunga' = mountain, 'kiekie' = a type of flax). The 183 m volcanic cone was the site of a major Maori pa, which once had a

population of 3000. The obelisk dedicated to the Maori people was unveiled by the Maori King, King Koroki, in 1948. The name One Tree Hill originally referred to the existence of a lone totara tree some hundreds of years old. This was destroyed in 1876 by a European settler who wanted firewood. A stand of pines planted as a replacement was thinned to a lone pine tree, which was cut down after being damaged in Maori protest attacks.

FROM TAMAKI DRIVE

Auckland Central, along the waterfront.

From car, bus or footpath, take in the harbour and islands from the pleasant waterfront drive which meanders 9 km from downtown Auckland to St Heliers Bay. Few cities have such lengthy, free public access to a waterfront drive and inner city beaches. Every year in March the annual Round the Bays Fun Run takes place along the road. Runners, walkers, people in wheelchairs, families and teams create crowds of up to 75,000 on the flat course. For a more considered view of the harbour and Rangitoto at any time, you can walk, bike or rollerblade along the footpath (several hire companies are along the route).

FROM THE SKY TOWER

Cnr Victoria and Federal Sts, Auckland Central.

Take a 40-second lift ride to the observation decks of the 328 m Sky Tower, highest tower in the Southern Hemisphere. Experience 360° panoramic views, operate touch screens with information about the sights you can see, and listen to a taped commentary.

The higher outdoor observation level is equipped with high-powered binoculars. The highest-level viewing platform, 'Skydeck', has seamless glass for an all-round view. The expanse of the Hauraki Gulf is particularly evident from here.

For a quirky view of this mighty engineering achievement, check the Sky Tower out from the base, looking straight up. Watch for jumpers descending on a bungy wire.

FROM THE TOP OF RANGITOTO ISLAND

The symmetry of Rangitoto comes from the lava flows which formed the volcanic island, beginning about 1000 years ago. Up close, the island terrain is much more jagged, but the view from the top is worth the effort. A walk to the summit is generally a two-hour return trip. Those with less time or energy can take a four-wheel-drive safari tour to a 900 m boardwalk at the base of the summit. See page 57 for further details.

FROM NORTH HEAD OR MT VICTORIA

Open: 7 days, vehicle access 8 am–8 pm (North Head), 8 am–8:30 pm (Mt Victoria), walking access 6 am–10 pm.

The view of the city from these two Devonport volcanic cones can be most spectacular at night. There's an imposing view of the classical Greek-style Auckland Museum (in 1929, the Auckland Electric Power Board paid the cost of the floodlighting so the war memorial museum 'should never be out of sight or mind'). Over the city, the winking lights you see are not stars, but the container lifters working 24 hours-a-day at the container port.

FROM THE TOP OF PIHA

The best view of a West Coast beach, black sand and boiling surf, is gained from the top of the Piha beach road, prior to its descent to Piha beach. Look for the famous lion rock and the long lines of surf that stretch up to North Piha.

FROM THE DEVONPORT FERRY

Close up and intimate shots of the harbour at work or pleasure are the stuff of the daily ferry commute from Auckland to

Devonport and back. Look for the naval base nearby as you arrive at Devonport. Sails every half hour, 15 minute trip, adult fares $8 return, children 5–15 yrs $4 return, under-5 yrs free, family pass $20 return for two adults and up to four children, or one adult and up to five children.

FROM THE NORTHERN APPROACH TO THE HARBOUR BRIDGE

The stretch of Northern Motorway from Takapuna to the Harbour Bridge offers the contrasting spectacle of the high clusters of city buildings across the harbour – best viewed at night, or at dawn – and the low groups of boats moored in the lee of Northcote Point and across Shoal Bay at the Bayswater Marina. As you descend the harbour bridge on the city side, the millions of dollars worth of yachts and launches tied up in the Westhaven marina to the left of the bridge underline Auckland's focus on harbour recreation.

FROM SCENIC DRIVE, WAITAKERE RANGES

A popular Sunday afternoon drive, and the road where sports coach Arthur Lydiard pioneered the celebrated long-distance training of New Zealand Olympic 800, 1500 and 5000 m gold medallists Peter Snell and Murray Halberg in the 1960s. Along the 30 km stretch, view the large Nihotupu dam (from the Arataki Visitor Centre, 6 km past Titirangi), distant vistas of Auckland city and the bush-covered valleys from roadside parks.

10 Top Beaches

From the flat, calm beaches of the inner city Waitemata harbour to the black-sand surf cauldrons of the West Coast, beaches in Auckland draw thousands of visitors for simple but characteristically New Zealand days of lazing, sunning and swimming. Within an easy drive there are dozens of beaches, but our pick of the 10 best contain a style of beach for everyone's tastes.

Mission Bay

Tamaki Dr, Mission Bay.

A white-sand beach, Mission Bay Reserve grassy area, and calm water provides an environment for safe and fun family swimming. There is a children's playground on site, picnic tables, coin-operated barbecue, and plenty of car parks. One of the most popular city beaches along the easily accessible waterfront drive (others further around include Kohimarama, and St Heliers Bay). After severe storm erosion, Mission Bay was refurbished at the cost of $2 million with 30,000 m³ of white sand transported from Northland. The shopping centre across the road includes nine restaurants in a row, from fast food to the exotic. Mission Bay Fountain and the historic Melanesian Mission House are added attractions.

Karaka Bay

Peacock St, Glendowie.

Descend from the smallest dead-end road off a busy suburban street (Riddell Road) in the eastern suburbs to reach this tiny hidden beach. Access by steps only. Enjoy the stylish beach-suburban houses of the few privileged enough to live at this shoreline gem. One resident likes it so much he brought his pet pig to live here!

Takapuna Beach

Access from side streets such as The Strand, or The Promenade off Hurstmere and Lake Rds, Takapuna. Long white sandy beach, calm water, spectacular dominant view of Rangitoto across the busy shipping lane of the Rangitoto Channel. Boats for hire. Popular walking beach, with access to Milford beach, north around the rocks at low tide. Boat ramp. Rock-pool marine life at the northern end are magnets for the children at low tide. Camping ground nearby, (Takapuna Beach Holiday Park, 22 The Promenade). Shops and restaurants are just a stroll away.

Cheltenham Beach

Cheltenham Rd.

Classic North Shore beach with close-up view of Rangitoto Island. Green foreshore adjacent to sand. Popular with walkers and those who enjoy their beaches less crowded. Safe swimming at high tide but a walk out to the sea at low tide. Handy to North Head promontory for those who like a bit of exercise and a view from the top with their day at the beach.

Long Bay

Beach Rd.

The 110 ha Long Bay seaside park is the busiest regional park in Auckland and has been developed around the most northerly of the North Shore beaches. It is 26 km from the city centre and reached by a regular bus service. The park has a firm, long, sandy beach, popular for swimming, and an extensive grassed area used especially by families and groups for recreation, picnics and barbecues. There is also a children's adventure playground. For those who prefer not to do-it-themselves, there's a local restaurant and beach shop. There is a coastal walk north through farmland and along cliff-tops to two smaller sandy bays. The park also offers mountain-bike routes.

Pt Chevalier

Pt Chevalier Rd and Harbour View Rd.

Easily accessible western suburbs beach with plenty of picnic areas, both in the green slopes that lead to the Harbour View Reserve side, and in Coyle Park above the smaller main Point Chevalier beach.

Piha

Piha Rd.

Popular black-sand and strong surf beach 45 km west of downtown Auckland city (surf-lifesaving patrols operate through summer). The beach is split in two by the huge reclining mass of Lion Rock. At the south of the beach 'the gap' produces fountaining surf through a blowhole. Swimming at Piha is recommended only in the areas patrolled by surf lifesavers as sea conditions can be hazardous. The name Piha means 'ripple at the bow of a canoe'. Episodes of the TV series *Xena, Warrior Princess* were filmed in the vicinity – and you thought those trees, bush and fern plants were native to ancient Roman times.

Karekare

Karekare Rd.

Wild west coast cousin of Piha, just next door, but preferred by some for its smaller, tougher character. Local surf lifesavers tell each other of their legendary swims around the rock out from the shore (experienced surf swimmers only), and visitors are in safe hands using the patrolled areas.

Karekare Falls along the beach is a taste of features found in the extensive walking and tramping track network that runs up into the surrounding Waitakere Ranges Regional Parkland. For many centuries Maori of the Kawerau iwi occupied the area, then came sawmillers and foresters (timber dams and remnants of railway lines moulder in the bush). Images of a Victorian grand piano sitting on the black sands of Karekare's pounding beach were iconic in Jane Campion's award-winning film *The Piano* (*Palme d'Or*, Cannes).

Muriwai

State Highway 16, then Muriwai Rd.

Another West Coast beach with yet a different character. Here the volcanic coastal cliffs surrounding Piha and Karekare give way to sand dunes as far as the eye can see. Stretching into the distance north towards the Kaipara Harbour, this black-sand beach attracts fishers for surfcasting and 4WD vehicles for a drive. Swimmers and sunbathers gather at the southern end of the beach.

Onetangi

The Strand.

Waiheke Island glamour spot. Sweeping white-sand beach where the slope gives you good swimming even at low tide, and the water temperature always seems a few degrees warmer than over on the mainland. Good bus service and taxi service from the Auckland ferry, bars for beachside recreation and a laid-back corner store/café where the big breakfasts are just the thing after an early morning swim.

Adventure

For those who like a bit of physical adventure, check out what will set your adrenalin pumping in Auckland city. For the gentler adventure-seeker, perhaps a sail or kayak paddle on the harbour will suit you better. Then you can have a latté or espresso at a café on the Viaduct, and watch the sun go down over the site of your endeavours.

AUCKLAND BRIDGE CLIMB

70 Nelson Street, Auckland Central, Ph: 377 6543.
Website: www.aucklandbridgeclimb.co.nz

Climb to the top of the Auckland Harbour Bridge (arch = 65 metres above the water) in a group led by a professional climb leader. This two-hour experience operates seven days a week (starting at 10 am and going every 20 minutes during the day), with a night climb on Saturday & Sunday. The experience includes being supplied with overalls and safety gear to put over your own clothes, a bus ride from the Auckland Bridge Climb city depot to the bridge, and a headset for the commentary. Participants need to wear rubber-soled shoes, be over seven years of age (a paying adult must accompany every two children up to 16 years old) and be more than 135 cm (4 ft 6 in) tall. The climb is suitable for all levels of fitness. No videos or cameras are allowed (climb leaders use their cameras to take photos of you or the view on your behalf) and no mobile phones. Cost, incl GST, is $125 per adult and $89 per child. And yes, one couple has already been married at the top of the bridge.

SKY TOWER JUMP

Sky Tower, Cnr Victoria and Federal Sts, Auckland Central, Ph: 0800 SKYJUMP (0800 759 586).

Website: www.skyjump.co.nz

Ever wanted to jump from a high tower like Superman and land safely? Well, adrenalin junkies in Auckland City do it from the 192 m tall Sky Tower, described as the highest land-based jump in the world. Not quite bungy jumping, but rather base-jumping – you are launched in a full body harness clipped by cable to a wire, to make a controlled 75 kmph 18-second descent, slowing down to a soft landing as the cable drum unrolls and meets air resistance. Open every day except Christmas day and New Year, last jump around dusk, for people over 10 years (written parental consent needed for children 10–13 years) in good health and under 120 kg. All equipment including jump suits supplied – wear suitable footwear. Cost is $195, incl GST. Student and backpacker concessions available.

Sky Tower jump.

GET OUT ON THE WATER

Get sailing in the City of Sails with one of the experienced yacht operators. If you ask you can even steer the boat. They say that the feeling you get when you hear the hiss of the water swishing past you while you are at the helm is something you will never forget.

Viking Cruises
Pier 3 Ticket Office, Quay St, Auckland City, Ph: 0800 SAIL NZ (0800 724 569).
Website: www.sailnz.co.nz

For two hours, you can imagine yourself at the heart of an America's Cup duel simply by getting aboard NZL40 and setting sail around the Auckland Harbour. The $NZ4 million NZL40 is a carbon-fibre hulled yacht, brought to New Zealand as a trial boat for the 1999/2000 America's Cup in Auckland, a contest won by New Zealand. The yacht has changed little from its original racing form, apart from extra safety requirements for passengers and diesel engines to save it having to be towed into the harbour.

Costs: 2hr racing $125 adults, $110 children; 3hr match racing in the weekends $195 adults, $175 children. Children 10–14 yrs must be accompanied by an adult and the trip is not recommended for children under the age of 10, pregnant women or people with a medical condition.

Pride of Auckland Yachts
New Zealand National Maritime Museum, Waterfront (near Viaduct Basin), Ph: 373 4557.
Website: www.prideofauckland.com

More than 30,000 visitors a year go for a gentle sail on the harbour on the Pride of Auckland yachts. Each 15 m yacht can take 21 passengers in comfort. The movement on the yachts is generally less than that experienced on an aeroplane flight, says the company, because sailboats don't fight nature but move with the wind in a steady motion. You could try the morning or afternoon straight cruises (45 minutes, $45 per adult $25 child [4–15 yrs] under 4 yrs free), or the coffee-and-muffin cruise (one and a half hours, $55 per adult, $30 per child), the luncheon cruise (one and a half hours, $65 per adult, $35 per child) or the evening dinner cruise (two and a half hours, $90 per adult, $55 per child). Wet-weather gear is provided and the fee includes entry to the Maritime Museum. Wear warm casual clothing.

Rangitoto Sailing
from The Landing on The Waterfront Drive, Ph: 358 2324.
Website: www.sailingnz.co.nz
Rangitoto Sailing, with the Royal Akarana Yacht Club operates a programme of per-hour or per-day sailing for casual visitors or for those who want to learn to sail. You sail with an experienced skipper aboard, and can visit nearby islands in the Hauraki Gulf such as Motuihe or Motukorea (Browns Island, a popular picnic destination for small boats), or simply slip along through the waves in the harbour breeze. There are six eight m Olympic Soling Class boats. Costs: 1–3 people, NZ$75 per hour, NZ$395 per 8hr day; 4 people, NZ$95 per hr, NZ$490 per 8hr day.

Soren Larsen
Princes Wharf West, next to the National Maritime Museum, Ph: 411 8755.
Website: www.sorenlarsen.co.nz
Take a sail on a 45 m 19th-century square-rigged brigantine, with oak hull and decking, traditional wooden masts and spars, 12 sails and a 7.8 m beam – wide enough for a walk across deck. The 300 tn ship hails from Denmark but is based in Auckland. During summer you can choose from a three-hour coffee (and scones) cruise for $57, a five-hour day-sail around the Hauraki Gulf (including a light lunch and a glass of wine) for $97, two, three and four-day expeditions around the Hauraki Gulf from $500–$900, or a five-day

cruise to the Bay of Islands for approx. $1200. Expect to steer, hoist a few sails and take part in duty watch on the longer cruises.

BALLOONING

Get away from it all, up, up and away in a beautiful balloon. Two companies offer roughly the same deal – a dawn flight of about an hour floating gently over the countryside followed by a champagne brunch. Flights operate all year (subject to weather conditions), generally at the weekends except during the busy season, which runs from Christmas until late March.

Balloon Safaris NZ Ltd
PO Box 300-065, Albany, Ph: 415 8289.
Website: www.balloonsafaris.co.nz
(subject to change) Costs: adults $250, children 8–13 years $175.
Flies mainly in the rural North Auckland area, south of Kaukapakapa and Orewa, but flights in the South Auckland area (south of Papakura and the Hunua Ranges) can be arranged.

Balloon Expedition Co of NZ Ltd
150 Moire Rd, West Harbour, Ph: 416 8590.
Costs: (subject to change) $230 per person.
Based in the north-west of Auckland. Flies around West Auckland, city and harbour. Bookings essential.

BUSHWALKING/TRAMPING

The Waitakeres are the closest large area of native bush in the Auckland region, and they offer fantastic tramping opportunities for adventurers. Companies tend to concentrate on gentle ambles, rather than heavy-duty tramping trips. The Arataki Visitor Centre (Ph: 817 0088), which is about 6 km past Titirangi along Scenic Drive, has plenty of information about walks and tramps in the area. But the weather is fickle, so be prepared: strong boots, warm clothing and waterproofs are essential, even on a fine day in summer.

CAVE VISIT

Nikau Cave, Waikaretu, RD 5, Tuakau, Ph: (09) 233 3199.
Website: www.nikaucave.co.nz

Anne and Phillip Woodward own a farm in Tuakau, 90 minutes south-west of Auckland where they run tours through a spectacular kilometre-long caving system on their property. If you don't mind getting a bit soggy and don't go all funny in confined spaces, you'll have an exhilarating time exploring this strange world of caverns and stalactites that have barely changed over thousands of years. It's full of glow-worms too. Two one-hour trips are available: one is a fairly physical scramble through the caves, emerging in native bush and a grove of nikau palms; the second is less demanding with visitors entering and exiting the main cave entrance. Costs: adults $20–25, children $12. Bring a change of clothing and footwear (footwear and overalls are available, and torches and helmets are provided). Bookings are essential.

CANYONING

Awol Canyoning Adventures Ltd
PO Box 56 207, Dominion Rd, Auckland, Ph: 834 0501.
Website: www.awoladventures.co.nz

Less of a canyon and more of a deep, long cleft in the earth, the Piha Canyon provides some fast-running streams, small waterfalls and caves for the adventurous to slide, jump and wander through – caves and jumps are optional for the less excitable. The pioneers herded giant kauri logs down this route and some of the old trees remain embedded in the canyon. No experience is required for this adventure, which is only a 40-minute drive from Auckland city near the thunderous West Coast beaches. Transport is provided from the city. Wetsuits, harnesses and helmets (and lunch) are provided. Full-day, half-day and night canyoning available.

CYCLING

Buy or hire a bike and see Auckland and its environs at your own pace. Dedicated cycle lanes are being created all the time, so look out for these safe riding zones beside the hurtling Auckland traffic. The motorways and the Harbour Bridge are no-cycle zones – catch the ferry if you want to get across the water to the North Shore.

Adventure Cycles
36 Customs St East, Auckland Central, Ph: 309 5566 or 0800 33 55 66.
Website: www.adventure-auckland.co.nz
Open: 7 days, 7 am–7 pm.
Touring/racing, mountain and tandem bikes available for hire on a daily, weekly or monthly basis from $18–$190. This company also sells bikes and will help organise cycle tours, eco tours and farm/home stays for travellers, and store your gear. They also guarantee to buy back bikes you have bought from them. Hireage includes helmet, lock, tool kit and water bottle, plus maps and tips. You can also hire panniers and bike trailers for luggage or the kids. If you choose a mountain bike, head first to Woodhill Forest in the north-west, which has kilometres of tracks dedicated to mountain biking, from the gentle to the downright hair-raising.

HORSERIDING

There's nothing like getting on a horse and going for a gallop. Different places cater for riders of varying ability, but all offer treks through some very scenic parts of the region – and none are more than one and a half hours' drive from Auckland.

Pakiri Beach Horse Riding
Rahuikiri Rd, Pakiri Beach. Ph: 0800 2 RIDE HORSE (0800 274 334).
Website: www.horseride-nz.co.nz
Open: 7 days (except Christmas Day).
Costs: 1 and 2-hour treks as well as half-day, full-day and overnight trips available, phone for prices.

A fantastic part of the world with a beautiful isolated beach. Treks on well-behaved horses will take you onto the beach, up through the sand dunes and pohutukawa forest, along the estuary and into the hills (depending on how long you go for). Other options include a seven-day coast-to-coast and a five-day warrior trail (which includes an overnight stay at a Maori marae).

South Kaipara Horse Treks & Riding Holidays
South Head, Helensville, Ph: (09) 420 2835.
Website: www.horserides.co.nz.
Costs: half-day trek $60, full-day trek $100 (includes lunch), overnight treks $300, multi-day treks $300 per day.

Rod and Bev Hedley specialise in taking groups of experienced riders for longer rides along the beaches of the Kaipara Harbour, through forests and farmland.

INDOOR KARTING

Climb into a go-kart and tear around the track to banish the day's frustrations. These stable, four-stroke karts (equipped with roll bars) have a top speed of 35 km per hour, but it feels much, much faster.

Trax Go-Karts
11 Industry Rd, Penrose, Ph: 525 2619.
Open: 6 Days, Tue to Fri 5 pm–10 pm, Sat noon–10 pm, Sun noon–8 pm.

Action Raceway
87 Small Rd, Silverdale, Ph: 09 426 1070.
Website: www.actionraceway.co.nz
Open: 7 days, 10 am–10 pm.

Extreme Indoor Kart Track
82B Kerwyn Ave, East Tamaki, Ph: 273 5552.
Open: 7 days, Mon to Fri noon–10 pm, Sat & Sun 10 am–10 pm.

INDOOR ROCK CLIMBING

This sport used to be limited to serious outdoor pursuiters who were afraid of nothing. Now it's quite the trendy thing among city types who want a good workout and a hefty dose of fear in their lives. It involves climbing into a harness, attaching ropes, and shinning up walls that have different shaped foot and hand holds. Another person on the ground, the belayer, controls your ropes so that, if you lose your grip, you won't plummet to the ground and ruin it for everyone else. Routes are of varying degrees of difficulty.

The RockNasium
610 Dominion Rd, Mt Eden, Ph: 630 5522.
Website: www.rocknasium.co.nz
Open: 7 days 10 am–10 pm except Christmas day, Boxing Day and New Year's day.
Costs: adults $20 unlimited time ($15 with own gear), includes basic instruction on belaying, harness and equipment; children under 15 years $15 ($10 with own gear).
Bookings essential for groups, or for extra climbing instruction. Offers walls for beginners through to advanced, and for kids to adults, set at different angles for varying degrees of difficulty.

Birkenhead Leisure Centre
Mahara Ave, Birkenhead, Ph: 418 4109.
Website: www.indoorrockclimbing.co.nz
Open: 7 days, Mon to Fri 9 am–10 pm, Sat to Sun 10 am–10 pm.
Costs: $13 adults for unlimited time (includes entry and harness), $10 (children under 15 yrs). Free instruction for beginners.

INLINE SKATING (ROLLERBLADING)

Look stylish as you glide along The Drive on your rollerblades ... or trip, stumble and fall like the rest of us! Mind the dogs and children, and keep to the path indicated.

Ferg's Inline Skate Hire
12 Tamaki Dr, Okahu Bay, Ph: 529 2230.
Website: www.fergskayaks.co.nz
Winter hours 9 am–6 pm, Summer hours 8 am–8 pm.
Costs: $10 for the first hour then $5 per hour after that; $25 all day (plus $5 overnight). Scooters also available for hire.

PAINTBALL

Paint gaming might be like war, but you're not allowed to call it that. It's PC to talk about 'tag' or 'laser' games, but that's the only subtle and sensitive thing about the sport. Basically, it involves running full tilt around a field or a two-storey darkened maze (depending on where you go) firing off rounds from your semi-automatic weapon with the aim of hitting the opposition with hard little blobs of paint. Any colour but red. Scores are kept on each player's special vest. Non-stop action. Expect to work up a bit of a sweat.

Action's Paintball
Cnr Pooks & O'Neill Rds, Swanson, Ph: 0800 321 228.
Website: www.actionspaintball.com
Open: 7 days, daylight hours.
Costs: $40 for a starter pack, which includes 100 paintballs.

LASER TAG

Same sort of game as Paintball, but laser guns are used and no paint is involved.

Megazone
15 Rose Rd, Ponsonby, Ph: 360 2900.
523A Ellerslie-Panmure Highway, Ellerslie, Ph: 570 7030.

79 Wairau Rd, Glenfield, Ph: 444 3423.

Website: www.megazone.co.nz

Open: 7 days, weekdays 3 pm–10 pm, weekends & public holidays 10 am–10 pm.

Costs: $8 per person for 15 minutes (fewer than 10 players); $6.50 per person (10 or more players).

PARACHUTING

If you're over 16, you can jump out of a plane strapped to an instructor! Once the terror of exiting a plane at 3500 m and freefalling for 1500 m (almost a minute) is over, you'll love the feeling of gliding in a controlled manner towards the ground. Alternatively, try a solo static-line jump from a large ram-air chute, which is very manoeuvrable and opens automatically after 3–4 seconds.

Skydive Parakai

Parakai Airfield, Greens Rd, Parakai, PO Box 146, Helensville (just 40 mins North of Auckland's CBD), Ph: 09 420 7327 or 0800 4A JUMP.

Tandem skydives offer you an opportunity to go totally wild, yet feel completely safe (these experienced hands have been throwing people out of planes since 1986). A jump makes a unique gift to loved ones, or treat yourself to an experience you'll never forget!

PARAGLIDING

If you have ever fancied running off a hill and soaring like a bird, this could be the adrenalin rush for you. It's pretty technical, but if you do a tandem flight, you don't have to worry about thermals and things. A one-day course will teach you all you need to know. Unlike parachuting, you can stay up for hours if you have the expertise.

SkyWings

35a Gollan Rd, Mt Wellington, Ph: 570 5757.

Website: www.skywings.co.nz

Costs: tandem flight $120, one-day introductory course $190.

Wings & Waves

4 Sir Peter Blake Pde, Bayswater, Ph: 446 0020 or 025 727 013.

Website: www.wingsandwaves.co.nz

Costs: tandem flight $120 for 20–30 minutes, one-day introductory course $190, kite-surfing lessons $160.

PARASAILING

Parasail Co

Mission Bay, Ph: 025 791 934.

Costs: $80 per person.

Here's the deal. You go out on a boat, get strapped into a harness with a chute attached, then get winched off a platform and suddenly find yourself airborne, being towed behind the boat. Apparently you can do somersaults, hang upside down, walk on water, fly around in circles or get dunked. Or you can do the whole thing without getting your feet wet. Then, when you're done, you get winched back onto the boat.

QUAD BIKING

There are 15,000 ha in the exotic pine Woodhill Forest (north-west of Auckland) and you can bump and roar along quite a few of them on a 300-cc quad bike (a four-wheeled farm bike). Riding one of these really is a blast. If you go for longer than one hour, you'll also get down to Muriwai Beach, a fabulous black-sand surf beach. All tours are fully guided and there's plenty of scope for shrinking violets as well as hooligans. Fifteen minutes of tuition is all you need. Safety helmets, goggles and gloves are provided. Twilight tours, combined helicopter and quad safaris can also be arranged.

4Track Adventures

Resthill Rd, Woodhill Forest, Ph: 0800 4 TRACK (0800 487 225), Ph: 420 8104.

Website: www.4trackadventures.co.nz

Costs: $115–135 per person for a one-hour guided safari, $175–195 for two hours, $215–235 for three hours.

SEA KAYAKING

See the harbour from sea level and at your own pace, and get some healthy exercise at the same time. Gentle trips across to Rangitoto Island if you fancy, including some at night. There are lots of paddling options: you can explore caves, propel yourself to islands in the Gulf, check out the northern regional parks by water or even canoe to the pub! Take your sandwiches and something to drink, unless food is provided, and don't forget a hat, sunglasses and sunscreen. Most companies won't take children or younger teenagers.

Ferg's Kayaks
12 Tamaki Dr, Okahu Bay, Ph: 529 2230.
Trips and costs: Rongitoto day or night trip, $75. Devonport/ North Head day or night trip, $75.

Outdoor Discoveries Ltd
PO Box 20-467, Glen Eden, Ph: 813 3399.
Website www.nzkayak.co.nz
Trips and costs: All types of trips catered for, from 'pub' trips to overnight excursions. See website or phone for up-to-date details.

Ross Sea Kayaking Adventures
11 Empire Ave, Enclosure Bay, Waiheke Island, Ph: 372 5550.
Website: www.kayakwaiheke.co.nz
Half-day guided tour, from Matiatia to the north-west corner of Waiheke island (ideal for beginners), $65. Full-day guided tour, paddle from Matiatia and return by shuttle, includes lunch, $125. Two/three day kayaking and camping around the eastern end of Waiheke, includes all meals, camping equipment, kayaks and island transport and return shuttle, phone to check latest trip details.

OUTDOOR ADVENTURE ORGANISATIONS

Auckland Adventures Ltd
PO Box 87-023, Meadowbank, Ph: 379 4545.
Website: www.aucklandadventures.co.nz

Offers three daily excursions around Auckland. Mountain bike adventure: full-day instructional downhill riding for all levels at Muriwai beach, $89, includes light refreshments. Wilderness adventure: full-day bushwalking and beach trip $89. Auckland adventure: half-day sightseeing, $60. All excursions include a visit to Mt Eden for a 360° view of Auckland, a trip to Muriwai beach, guided tour of the gannet colony, a visit to an orchard and winery where visitors can enjoy a free wine-tasting. Groups can opt to camp overnight.

Cliffhanger Training & Adventures Ltd
PO Box 15-343, New Lynn, Auckland, Ph: 827 0720.
Website: www.cliffhanger.co.nz
Costs: range from $45 to $495.

More high-adrenalin fun, including abseiling/rappelling, outdoor education, outdoor rock climbing, sea kayaking, tramping/hiking.

Wanderwomen
PO Box 68 058, Newton, Ph: 360 7330.
Website: www.wanderwomen.co.nz
Costs: day trips from $55, weekends from $250, five-day trips from $535.

Adventure tours for women, specialising in abseiling/rappelling, rock climbing, sea kayaking, multi-activity weekends and challenge courses, operating year-round. Scare yourself stupid and bond with the other girls.

CRUISING/CHARTER BOATS

For a full charter trip either with a skipper included or operating the boat yourself, there are plenty of charter companies available. Check the telephone directory Yellow Pages for contact details (website: www.yellowpages.co.nz).

Island-hopping

It's impossible to spend time in Auckland and be unaware of the fact that the city is framed by the Hauraki Gulf, and that the Gulf is full of islands. There are 47 in total – from the large 'commuter suburb' of Waiheke to a number of named rocks that poke up out of the ocean. You can visit the recreation islands by public transport, or moor a yacht in their harbours, while the conservation islands have been set aside as sanctuaries for struggling plant and animal populations – especially birds – and access to them is restricted. Special permits are required to visit some islands, and others are completely out of bounds.

WAIHEKE

Waiheke is the largest island in the inner Gulf and has a population of over 7000, including many commuters to the mainland – a manageable 35 minutes away by ferry. Home to many artists and craftspeople, it always had a reputation as a hippy hideout, but in summer, the population swells to an amazing 30,000 people, all wanting to take advantage of Waiheke's food, wine and holiday fun.

Waiheke was originally settled by Maori around 1200 AD and traces of an old fortified Maori settlement, or pa, can be seen on the headland overlooking Putiki Bay. The missionary Samuel Marsden brought Europeans to the island in the early 1800s and it was stripped of its kauri forest soon afterwards.

It's a little warmer and drier than the mainland, and the glorious white sandy beaches of Oneroa, Palm Beach and

Onetangi are great for swimming, fishing, snorkelling and scuba diving. Beetle around Waiheke's coast in a charter yacht or in a sea kayak.

Back on land, you can go tramping (hiking) in bush or over farmland, set off on a horse trek, play a round of golf, hire a mountain bike or scooter, picnic, camp or check out the craft shops and vineyards. Check out options on www.waiheke.co.nz or www.aucklandnz.com

Waiheke Visitor Information Service

2 Korora Rd, Oneroa, Waiheke Island, Ph: 372 1234.

Situated in Oneroa, Waiheke's main settlement, the office is open daily. It's a free local phone call from Auckland.

GETTING THERE

Fullers Auckland

Ferry Building, Quay St, Auckland Central, Ph: 367 9111. The Waiheke Island Info-phone number (information about sailings and prices) is: 367 9119. Website: www.fullers.co.nz

Costs (direct, return): adults $24, children $12 (under-fives are free), family $59.

Fullers' Island Explorer tour includes the ferry ride and a one and a half hour commentated scenic highlights bus trip. Costs: adults $46, children $22.50. A vineyard tour (adults $66) and Beyond and Back tour (adults $47, children $25) are also available.

Subritzky Shipping Line Ltd

Half Moon Bay, Pakuranga, Infoline Ph: 534 5555.

Website: www.subritzky.co.nz

Operates four vehicle ferries that carry up to 30 cars and 200 passengers. Advance bookings essential. Costs: $106 return for a medium-sized car, $24 per adult return, $12 per child, under-fives are free.

Great Barrie

Waiheke

Mission House, Kawau.

Tiritiri Matangi.

GREAT BARRIER (AOTEA)

'The Barrier' has always had a wild, pioneering side to it. This is a huntin', shootin', fishin' island, but it has a softer side and some fascinating characters call it home. There are about 1200 residents in its 285 km² and it is great for tramping (hiking), swimming, scuba diving, surfing, sea kayaking, fishing, cycling and relaxing in the hot springs. Like Waiheke, there are no introduced grazing pests such as possums or deer, so the native bush is lush.

Great Barrier was inhabited by Maori when Captain Cook came in 1769 and gave the island its English name. It became a whaling centre, many kauri trees were felled for timber and kauri gum digging was important for a time. It was the first place in the world to have an airmail postal service (in 1897). Many ships have come to grief around the Barrier's rugged coast, and victims of the *Wairarapa* (which went down in 1894) are buried in the cemetery in Katherine Bay in the north.

Great Barrier has no towns. Tryphena is the main settlement, with a few dozen houses and several shops. Port Fitzroy is the other 'big smoke' – with a Department of Conservation office (Ph: 09 429 0044). The airport is at Claris as is the information centre. There is no electricity supply on the island: power is supplied by generator, wind turbine or solar panels. Everyone has their own water supply and most roads are unsealed. There are no banks, though some outlets offer EFTPOS. Not the place for lounge lizards or cappuccino addicts. You can hire a car (from about $50 a day), or a bike (around $25 a day) or just walk around taking in the scenery. See Department of Conversation's track information leaflet on the island's walks and tramps.

slands of the Hauraki Gulf

sit recreation islands by ferry or
ht aircraft, or moor a yacht in
eir harbours. Regular ferries run
Rangitoto, Motuihe, Waiheke
d Great Barrier Island from the
rry Building at the bottom of
ueen Street. To get to Kawau
and take the ferry from
andsworth, Warkworth.

Sandspit

Mahurangi

Waiwera

Orewa

Long
Bay

North
Shore

Waiheke Island

Hooks
Bay

Owhiti
Bay

Stony Batter

Oneroa
ackpool
Ostend
Onetangi
Surfdale
Omiha
Awaawaroa
Bay
Omaru
Bay

Auckland
City

Hauraki Gulf

Kawau Bay
North Cove
Kawau
Island
Bon Accord Harbour
Mullet Point
■ Mansion House
South Cove
Kawau
Point

Manukau
Harbour

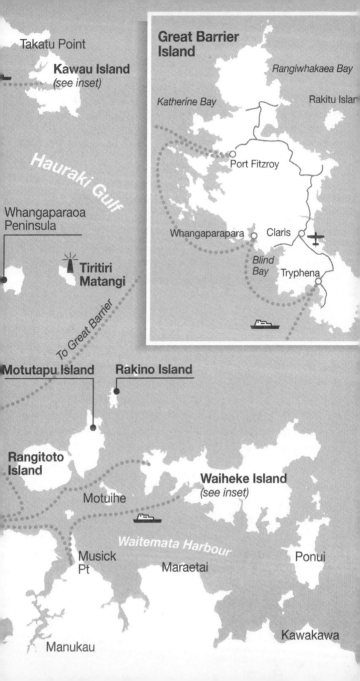

GETTING THERE

Fullers Auckland
Ferry Building, Quay St, Auckland Central, Ph: 367 9111.
Website: www.fullers.co.nz

The Great Barrier Island info-phone number (recorded information about sailings and prices) is Ph: 367 9117.

Subritzky Shipping Line
43 Jellicoe St, Auckland Central, Ph: 373 4036 or Infoline Ph: 534 5555.
Website: www.subritzky.co.nz

These vessels leave from Auckland's Wynyard Wharf 5 times a week, carrying a mix of vehicles, people and most of the island's freight. The trip takes around 3 hours, food and drinks are available on board. Advance bookings are required.

Great Barrier Airlines
Ph: 275 9120.
Website: www.greatbarrierairlines.co.nz

This airline flies all over the top of the North Island, but most often between Auckland and Claris on the Barrier. Flights to Claris depart Auckland daily at 7.45 am, 10.15 am and 4 pm, for $172 adult return and $110 child return. A shuttle bus meets these flights and drops off in Medlands and Tryphena. Charter flights can be arranged.

Great Barrier Xpress
Mountain Air, Auckland Airport, Ph: 256 7025.
Website: www.mountainair.co.nz

Regular scheduled flights from Auckland Airport to the Barrier are daily at 7.45 am and 9.00 am. Costs (return): adults $174, children $114.

RANGITOTO

Rangitoto Island, 260 m above sea level at its summit, is the largest and youngest of Auckland's 50 volcanoes. Local Maori are thought to have watched the island erupt into life around 600 years ago, as human and dog footprints have been found in ash hardened into rock on Rangitoto's near neighbour, Motutapu. It last erupted around 250 years ago and almost the entire surface of the island is lava. There are more than 200 different plant species on the island, including 40 varieties of fern.

Devonport Borough Council once leased out camping sites, but today the island is a public domain administered by Department of Conversation, which is responsible for controlling possum numbers and maintaining the tracks, signs, wharves and facilities. The wharves at Rangitoto and Islington Bays are for commercial use only.

Anyone can visit the island. It's a great place for a picnic, a hike up to the summit for extraordinary views of the region, a swim in the saltwater swimming pool by the wharf or a look around the lava caves. The walk to the summit takes about an hour and you can do a loop walk around the rim of the crater. The lava caves walk is a 30-minute detour. There are several other walks into the interior or around the coast, from short strolls to the two and a half hour return walk to Islington Bay.

Pounding up to the top on a blazing summer's day can take its toll, though. Sunlight reflects off the black rock, making it very hot. Always take plenty of water with you, wear a hat and sunscreen and leave your strappy high heels at home. Bring food as well, as there is none on the island.

GETTING THERE

Fullers ferries run a regular service. Costs are $20 per adult and $10 per child or $50 for a family pass. Check the Fullers

Infoline, Ph: 367 9120 for details of sailings and Explorer tours which will take you to the summit or around the island in the comfort of a dinky 4WD road train.

MOTUTAPU

Motutapu (or 'Sacred Island') is a very different piece of land to its close neighbour, Rangitoto. (A causeway between the two islands was built during World War II.) It looks like a farm in the middle of the Gulf, which, essentially, it is. Sheep and cattle graze there, but large tracts are being set aside for environmental regeneration. Motutapu was bought from the Maori in 1842 for 10 empty casks, 4 double-barrelled shotguns, 50 blankets, 5 hats, 5 pieces of material, 5 shawls and 5 pairs of black trousers.

During World War II, it was taken over for military purposes (as was Rangitoto). Six-inch coastal defence guns and radar were used to watch for the enemy and there was also an underground operations room. The entrances to the tunnels can still be seen dotted about on the hillsides.

Boaties and yachties can anchor at Home Bay and the western edge of Administration Bay. Watch out for reefs. Ferry sailings and costs are as for Rangitoto.

KAWAU

Kawau Island, east of Warkworth is dominated by the gracious Mansion House homestead, home of Governor George Grey who bought Kawau in 1862 for £3700. He enlarged and renovated an existing house and spent many years entertaining distinguished visitors here. It was run as a guesthouse for 57 years from 1910 before being sold to the government and eventually restored. It is open to the public daily. The grounds around the house are noted for their exotic plants and wildlife, a legacy from Governor Grey's time.

The island was the site of one of New Zealand's earliest

mining ventures in the 1840s. You can see remains of the copper mines if you go on a short bush walk from the homestead. Other good walks include the Redwood Track (one hour return), the Sunny Bay track, Harris Bay track and Schoolhouse Bay Road.

There are wharves at South Cove, Mansion House Bay and School House Bay for boaties and there is safe anchorage at Bon Accord Harbour and North Cove Harbour.

GETTING THERE

Kawau Kat Cruises
Viaduct Wharf, Auckland Central and Sandspit, Warkworth, Ph: 0800 888 006.
Website: www.kawaukat.co.nz
From Auckland, the Paradise Cruise trip takes two hours and leaves daily at 9.30 am during summer. The return boat leaves Kawau at 3 pm. Costs (return): adults $59, children $24, including a BBQ lunch on board. From Sandspit, the Royal Mail Run leaves at 10.30 am throughout the year. The catamaran visits each bay delivering mail and goods to residents and also stops at Mansion House. Costs (return including lunch): adults $49, children $18.

Matata Cruises
Sandspit, Warkworth, Ph: 0800 225 292 or after hours Ph: 09 425 6169.
This company runs a choice of two cruises to Kawau, a luncheon cruise with lunch and wine served on board and a coffee cruise with time on shore at Mansion House Bay.

TIRITIRI MATANGI

This is an exceptional spot, one of the very few places in the country where you can still be deafened by birdsong. An open sanctuary 4 km off the coast of the Whangaparaoa Peninsula, wildlife here is protected but visitors are permitted. You are NOT allowed to bring any form of vermin, so leave your ferret, cat, dog, stoat or possum at home. Native birds, including many rare species, are doing extremely well here and the takahe are so tame they are like pets. Other species include stitchbirds, saddlebacks, black robins, bellbirds, parakeets, whiteheads and little spotted kiwi, as well as common species such as tui and fantails.

In addition to thriving bird populations, over 250,000 locally propagated native trees have been planted on the island by thousands of volunteers.

There is an information office and shop by the lighthouse, which is New Zealand's best-preserved historic lighthouse complex, consisting of a signal station, several fog-horns and two cottages. No food is available but boxed lunches can be provided if ordered when booking.

Boaties and yachties should note that there are no areas allocated for berthing.

GETTING THERE

Fullers run summertime trips from Thursday to Sunday departing from Auckland at 9 am and from Whangaparaoa (Gulf Harbour) at 9.45 am. Costs (return) from Auckland: adults $45, children $23. From Whangaparaoa (return): adults $25, children $15. A guided ramble on the island is only an extra $5 donation per person. Ph: 367 9111 to book.

MOTUIHE

Motuihe, another Department of Conservation recreational reserve within the Hauraki Gulf Maritime Park, lies halfway between Auckland and Waiheke. Its full name, Motu a Ihenga ('the island of Ihenga'), commemorates the visit made to the island by Ihenga, an ancestor of the Arawa tribe, in the 14th century. Fortified pa, open settlements, karaka groves, cultivations and food storage pits are still visible.

The island came into European hands in 1839, when it was made over to farmland.

A human quarantine station was established on the northern headland in 1874 when smallpox was discovered on a boat visiting Auckland. It operated until 1929. Victims of the 1918 influenza epidemic are buried here. During World War I, it became a prisoner-of-war camp.

There are some lovely beaches on the northwest peninsula for today's visitors to explore, and there are also a number of walking tracks. It takes about three hours to circum-navigate the whole island.

GETTING THERE

Check with the Fullers for details, Ph: 367 9111. Website: www.fullers.co.nz

RAKINO

Rakino is one of the less well-known of Hauraki's islands. It lies slightly to the north of Motutapu and was originally known as Hurakia. Purchased from the Maori in 1840, a twist of fate saw it accommodate prisoners taken during the New Zealand Wars just a couple of decades later. Today it is mostly privately owned, with 10 ha being Department of Conversation recreation reserve. With sandy beaches and a rugged coastline, it's a good place for a day trip.

For boaties, there is a wharf at Sandy Bay and safe anchorage at West Bay, Woody Bay, Home Bay and Sandy Bay in reasonable weather conditions.

GETTING THERE

The island is on one of Fullers inner gulf mail runs. Ph: 367 9111 or try www.fullers.co.nz.

Fun and Free

WANDER THE REGIONAL PARKS

Auckland is proud of its more than 37,000 hectares of regional parks, from grassy beachside areas to farmland and on to the bush-covered Waitakere and Hunua ranges on the fringes of the city.

Try Wenderholm, Auckland's first regional park just north of the city where you can check out a special grove of pohutukawa trees; or the Regional Botanic Gardens on Hill Road just off the Southern Motorway at Manurewa – where 65 hectares have been planted with 30,000 native shrubs, plants and flowers.

To the west of the city the sprawling Waitakere Ranges Regional Parkland offers more than 16,000 ha of native forest and coastline, including over 200 km of walking and tramping tracks as well as the West Coast beaches. Start at the Arataki Nature Trail (Arataki Visitors Centre, 6 km along the Scenic Drive from Titirangi). Descend down a gentle slope on a 500 m walk where giant kauri and tagged native plants give you a sense of the look of native flora. To the south of the city, Hunua Regional Parkland has Auckland's largest forested landscape. Four dams in the ranges supply the greater part of Auckland's water. Check out the walking tracks, lookout spots with stunning views, and the Hunua Falls. For more information, phone ParksLine on Ph: 303 1530.

PICNIC

Grab your own style of food and head to any of many free and pleasant sites, including:

The Auckland Domain, Park Rd, Auckland Central. On the hill in front of the museum – great harbour views.

Victoria Park, Beaumont St, Auckland Central. On the grass beside the free pétanque court – watch, or if you have the boules, play (rules are up on a board).

Mt Hobson Domain, Remuera Rd, Remuera. Climb the (small) mountain, and get the view from the northern slopes of wealthy Remuera home owners.

Takapuna Beach, from side streets off Hurstmere Rd, Takapuna. Swim or gaze at Rangitoto and the passing shipping.

Cornwall Park, Manukau Rd, Royal Oak. Children's playground, plenty of trees and grass, explore more than 100 ha. Around the other side of the park (drive through, or use Pohutukawa Dr entrance, off Greenlane Rd West) find barbeques ready-stacked with council-supplied wood.

Omana Regional Park. Walk the farm, feed the chickens, picnic under the trees.

Auckland Regional Botanic Gardens, 102 Hill Rd, Manurewa. Plenty of picnic tables among the 30,000 plants and 10 ha of native bush.

Myers Park. Central city peace a few metres away from central city shopping. Asian foods available over the road in the varied shops along the upper reaches of Queen St.

Albert Park, access from Victoria St East or Princes St. Take a break from city sightseeing and join students lunching in the sun on the grass.

FEED THE BIRDS

Western Springs lake (Great North Rd, Western Springs) – ducks, geese, swans, pukeko.

The pond at the Auckland Domain (Park Rd, Auckland Central) – ducks.

Omana Regional Park (Omana Beach Rd, off Maraetai Drive, Maraetai) – chickens.

Lake Pupuke (Killarney St, Takapuna) – ducks, swans.

WATCH THE PLANES LAND AND TAKE OFF

Park in the Puhinui Road free viewing area (500 m east of the airport, open 5 am–10 pm). Busy air traffic peaks at around 7 am, 12–1 pm and 5–7 pm Mon, Tues, Thurs or Fri, and Sat around 7 am, depending on air traffic control schedules. Alternatively, there are good viewing areas in Auckland Airport terminals.

ENJOY

The coloured waters of the Mission Bay fountain playing at night. The charming display was devised and engineered more than 50 years ago. In the days before television, parents used to take their young children to watch from parked cars beside the Mission Bay reserve in the evening.

READ FOR FREE

Auckland Central Public Library, Lorne St, Auckland Central.
Open Mon to Fri 9.30 am–8 pm, Sat 10 am–4 pm, Sun 12 pm–4 pm.
Catch up with latest magazines and newspapers as well as books. Newspaper reading room is on the second floor. For the other 16 free libraries around the city, check the phone book under Auckland City Council.

VISIT

The Auckland Museum
Free, as ruled under the Auckland War Memorial Act 1996 for access to the war halls of remembrance, but for the general museum a donation is requested ($5 suggested). See 'Top 20 Attractions', p. 105.

TOUR

The Port for Free
See the port at work from a free public boat tour. Every Wednesday at 11 am, Ports of Auckland run a one-hour cruise that takes you alongside the container terminals where you can see the big cranes at work. A running commentary will also tell you about the general wharves, Westhaven Marina and the Viaduct Harbour. Tours leave from Pier 3 at the Ferry Building, Quay St. To book Ph: 367 9111.

40 Top Restaurants

**_Viva_'s Guide to the Best of Auckland Restaurants
By Ewan McDonald**

Okay, so we lost the America's Cup. But Auckland kept the
Viaduct Harbour, its waterfront playground. Five years ago
there was nothing here but a few dilapidated wharves where
fishing boats tied up: now it is a pulsating eating, drinking
and partying precinct. Alongside, Princes Wharf boasts cool
bars, restaurants and the Hilton, sailing into Waitemata
Harbour like a cruise liner. At the Hilton's White restaurant,
diners sit above the water, drink fine New Zealand wines and
eat superb local food, served with a dash of patriotism now
that Kiwi Geoff Scott has replaced Aussie superstar Luke
Mangan as executive chef at the flagship eatery. Up the hills
from the harbour, locals can also thank the Cup for the most
exciting new eatery in town: superstar chef Simon Gault was
computer billionaire Larry Ellison's personal cook aboard his
superyacht until he walked the plank and launched
sensational Gault@George in Parnell. In genteel Herne Bay,
one of the city's favourite dining-rooms has undergone a
metamorphosis. Canadian megadollars enticed Prue Barton
and David Griffiths to a start-of-the-art winery in Hawke's
Bay: the couple still own the scintillating Vinnie's but have

turned the kitchen over to their protégé, Michael Meredith. In boho Ponsonby, Paula Macks and Chris Rupe opened reputedly the city's most expensive makeover, luscious Chandelier, serving modern takes on Italian traditions. Just a 15-minute ferry ride across the harbour from downtown, the elegant 100-year-old Esplanade Hotel welcomes daytrippers. On a sunny day, what could rival the 40-minute voyage to Waiheke for lunch, perhaps at a winery? Or a drive to Henderson to relax among the vines? Don't feel, though, that you have to suit up and pay dearly for Auckland's best cuisine. The heart and soul of the city's dining can be found in its quirky cafes, casual coffee-shops and ethnic eateries. Enjoy!

For the most up-to-date dining news and reviews, read the NZ Herald's *Viva* section on Wednesdays or visit www.nzherald.co.nz/restaurants. Ewan McDonald is *Viva*'s restaurant reviewer.

NORTH RESTAURANTS

The Dining Room
Spencer on Byron Hotel, 9–17 Byron Ave, Takapuna, Ph: 916 4982
Website: www.spencerbyron.co.nz

Pacific Rim cuisine, based on seasonal produce, from a kitchen that won 5 medals at the National Salon Culinaire 2003 lift this contemporary hotel restaurant above the average (and, sadly, there are some very average establishments around this laidback, beachy suburb).

Esplanade Hotel
1 Victoria Rd, Devonport, Ph: 445 1291.
Website: www.esplanadehotel.co.nz

There's something very Agatha Christie about this dining room since its renovation a couple of years ago . . . damask tablecloths and napkins, chandeliers, 1920-ish light opera and jazz. But the food is modern, as chef Paul Watson offers a grazing menu of interesting and extravagant fusion dishes, suggesting that diners try several smaller tastes rather than a conventional entrée-main-dessert meal.

K'St Restaurant (formerly Killarney Street Brasserie)
2 Killarney St, Takapuna, Ph: 489 9409.
Website: www.killarneyst.co.nz

The name and ownership change hasn't altered anything: Takapuna's icon brasserie has been packing the punters on to its sea-view deck every afternoon, and massive, casual restaurant every night, for over 10 years. The food and wine lists are extensive but if you're subject to panic attacks when faced with too much choice stick to what K'St does best: ex-Soul chef Michael Berry's straightforward steaks and panfried, blackened, baked or beer-battered fish.

PONSONBY, HERNE BAY, GREY LYNN

Chandelier
152 Ponsonby Rd, Ph: 360 9315.

Chris Rupe and Paula Macks' SPQR cafe next door has been the hippest place in town for a decade. Their new, drop-dead posh restaurant boasts Marcel Leydesdorff's light, fresh take on classical Italian. The classical Monacan, Prince Albert, is reported to have enjoyed the nosh when he was in town for the America's Cup.

Craft
551 Richmond Rd, Grey Lynn, Ph: 376 5595.
Website: www.craft.net.nz

Industrial décor, sometimes bleak choice in music, warmed by enthusiastic service, a savvy winelist and extraordinary choice of tapas or more substantial fare. Subtle, passionate inspirations of flavour and texture by Pip Wylie, once of London's Sugar Club, River Café and Point 5 Nine in a relaxed, chatty and bohemian atmosphere. No bookings, so you may have to wait at the bar for a table. Life could be worse.

Prego
226 Ponsonby Rd,
Ph: 376 3095.

Afternoon: antipasti on the terrace. Evening: pizza or a grill with chianti inside. You can't go past every Ponsonbyite's second home (believe us, we've tried) because it is consistently good, reasonably priced, and has been so for the past 15 years. Okay, so it gets noisy, overcrowded and chaotic – but so does Italy.

Red
170 Jervois Rd, Herne Bay,
Ph: 376 5367.

If you don't have a good time, don't blame your host. Kal Bouhdoud comes from Morocco and his ebullient welcome sets the tone for this lively, unpretentious restaurant right next door to one of the country's finest diners, Vinnie's. The menu comes from Italy with a dash of Southern France but on winter Sundays Kal throws his chef out of the kitchen and cooks tagine, the rich casseroles of his homeland.

Rocco
23 Ponsonby Rd,
Ph: 360 6262.

Fresh, lusty, Spanish-inspired food. Intelligent wine list with some surprises. Two of the most charming hosts you could hope to encounter, Blair Russell and Mark Wallbank. Young, upbeat, on-to-it staff . . . and a surprisingly laidback atmosphere.

Vinnie's
166 Jervois Rd, Herne Bay, Ph: 366 5597.

Website: www.vinnies.co.nz

How's this for a reference: Gordon Ramsay loves this restaurant. And if you can satisfy one of the world's best and most cantankerous cooks, you must be doing everything right. Vinnie's stands for elegance and under-statement; for utter attention to detail; for honest food using the best of produce, conceived by executive chef David Griffiths and executed by his man in the kitchen, Michael Meredith.

PARNELL, EASTERN SUBURBS

Antoine's
333 Parnell Rd, Parnell, Ph: 379 8756.

Website: www.antoinesrestaurant.co.nz

Tony and Beth Astle are celebrating 30 years at this stately institution. Astle hosts royalty, world leaders, international celebrities at what has been called 'the most exclusive and elite restaurant in the country.' He de-scribes his food as NZ cuisine with French undertones and runs two menus: Nostalgia has long-time favourites like oxtail casserole, braised lamb shanks, creamy tripe, bread-and-butter pudding; the Weekly is more contemporary. The wine list is breathtaking.

Bell House

Lloyd Elsmore Park, Bells Rd Pakuranga, Ph: 577 1330.

Website: www.halfmoonbayrestaurant.co.nz

Auckland's colonial history is immortalised in this 150-year-old British army officer's home, part of the Howick Historical Village in the city's well-heeled eastern suburbs. The menu is a subtly updated riff on old-time favourites: lamb, steaks, pork, venison and seafood.

Cibo

Axis Building, 91 St Georges Bay Rd, Parnell, Ph: 303 9660.

Website: www.cibo.co.nz

Kate Fay, the resident chef and genius, mixes exotic and familiar ingredients into honest, passionate food. The vintages hail from every nook and vineyard of the civilised world. Service is professional and charming. What more could you want? How about a gorgeous, mirrored and furred interior or an outdoor piazza in the midst of a 30-style chocolate factory turned apartment-office complex?

Gault @ George
144 Parnell Rd, Parnell, Ph: 358 2600.
Website: www.georgerestaurant.co.nz

Less than a year old, this has matured into the most exciting restaurant in Auckland. Diners lap up the ingenious concoctions of superstar chef Simon Gault and sidekick Shane Yardley in a generously proportioned Georgian room presided over by the city's suavest maitre d', Robert Johnson, and are seduced by a stunning cellar.

Halo
425 Tamaki Drive, St Heliers, Ph: 575 9969.
Website: www.halorestaurant.co.nz

Guy Malyon created the city's best suburban bistro at One Tree Grill, then subtly updated a tired brasserie into a very good, very grown-up restaurant across the road from the sparkling Waitemata Harbour. Simon Moss also oversees this menu, slightly more conservative than OTG's, uses ingredients and combinations that have become familiar over the past few years and relies on sauces to give them a kick.

Number 5

5 City Rd, Ph: 309 9273.

Website: www.number5.co.nz

Number 5 was, until midyear, a wine-lover's haven with an excellent kitchen. In recent months owner Martina Lutz has gone back to the kitchen, ditched the country-comfort food for a more grown-up menu and lifted it into the clique of Auckland restaurants that can be said to offer refined dining, while John Ingle's encyclopaedic knowledge of NZ wines and winemaking enlivens and elevates any visit.

Thai Friends Restaurant

311 Parnell Rd, Parnell, Ph: 373 5247.

Website: www.thaifriends.co.nz

Just as the British have adopted curry as their national dish, so young Kiwis have embraced Thai cuisine – often following their back-packing adventures in Asia. Here, Pad Thai (stir-fried noodles with chicken, shrimp, bean sprout, spring onion and crushed peanuts) is the specialty of the house. It's hard to fault anything else on the vast menu. Or the service, the Thai beers, the courtyards and the traditional dining-room downstairs . . .

TriBeCa

The Foundation Building, 2/8 George St, Ph: 379 6359.

Website: www.tribeca.co.nz

It takes its name from New York, its décor from a Merchant-Ivory movie, its wines from New Zealand's most prestigious vineyards, mostly in Hawkes Bay, and its food from everywhere. Throughout the year Richard Harris will tinker with ideas from Thailand, the Middle East, Europe and the Americas; he is also that rarity in Auckland, an accomplished dessert chef.

Veranda Bar and Grill

279 Parnell Rd, Ph: 309 6289.

Website: www.vbg.co.nz

Home of the Slow Food Movement in the city, Andrew Bell's 'VBG' offers familiar and reliable comfort food in pleasant surroundings: Thai chicken curry, bangers and mash, chicken, lamb shanks, duck with noodles, and a good selection of local and international wines. Those who like to eat later than Auckland's early-ish closing hours should keep it in mind.

CITY RESTAURANTS

Ariake
Corner Albert & Quay Sts,
Ph: 379 2377.
Website: www.ariake.co.nz

Auckland has long celebrated its place on the Pacific Rim: 20 and more years ago Ariake was one of the city's original Japanese restaurants. If this style of dining is unfamiliar, get to know it through set meals or the Ariake Dinner, a 10-course voyage through Japanese food. Service is polite and discreet.

Ding How
55 Albert St, CBD,
Ph: 358 4838.

Don't take our word for it: The NZ-China Society hosts visiting delegations at this lively, intimate Cantonese restaurant. It may not have the flash of many recent arrivals in town but we reckon it's one of the best yum cha places around. Don't restrict yourself to the usual suspects – try the fried prawns, spicy crab and fried squid tentacles.

Euro Restaurant and Bar
Shed 22, Princes Wharf, Ph: 309 9866.

Michael James has revitalised this waterside bistro since he arrived in the kitchen midyear, turning out imaginative, considered fusion. Previous visitors will be heartened to see that there is a special

page on the menu for 'signature dishes', favourites from the four years that the place has been around, like the flashest steak sandwich in the city.

Kermadec Ocean Fresh Restaurant
Cnr Quay & Lower Hobson Sts, Viaduct, Ph: 309 0412.

Website:
www.kermadec.co.nz

The only waterfront restaurant where there's no problem getting a park – you just steer your superyacht into the Viaduct marina and tie up right out front. As you'd expect from the site, go there for expertly crafted and rigidly executed seafood. It's a sizeable operation with 2 restaurants, 3 bars, 2 private Tatami rooms and a private function area.

Mikano

1 Solent St, Mechanics Bay, Ph: 309 9514.

Website: www.mikano.co.nz

Jonah Lomu and the All Blacks celebrated the big guy's wedding here, and we're not about to argue with those blokes. Established in 1994, John Flack keeps the customers satisfied with old favourites (fish cooked any of five ways, pork cutlets) while putting his own stamp on beautifully presented presentations of simple, seasonal flavours. Oh, and you can park your helicopter at the door.

Orbit

Sky Tower, Cnr Federal & Victoria Sts, Ph: 363 6000 or 0800 SKYCITY.

Website: www.skycity.co.nz

Uh-huh, you're thinking, 'tourist trap.' You couldn't be more wrong. Keith McPhee is one of the country's premier chefs, helming waterfront icons Cin Cin and The Esplanade in Auckland and Shed 5 in Wellington. His food is worthy of its place atop one of the tallest buildings south of the Equator. Service, however, can be dizzy.

O'Connell St Bistro
3 O'Connell St, Ph: 377 1884.
Website: www.menus.co.nz

Small but perfectly formed, this gorgeous little restaurant has just 12 tables; a proprietor, Chris Upton, trained in the UK, with 4 years' experience on the QE2; and a head chef, Sean Armstrong, a Kiwi who has worked in the kitchens like the Michelin-starred Green House in London. They will have to expand one day to find more room for international awards from people like the New York Wine Spectator. Upton and Armstrong also run Prime, the upmarket lunch venue in the Pricewaterhousecooper Tower, Quay St.)

Otto's
Metropolis Building, 40 Kitchener St, Ph: 300 9595.
Website: www.ottos.co.nz

Elegant, sophisticated, and beautifully managed. Four years ago *Viva* was the first to name it Auckland's best restaurant; it has faltered only occasionally and returned to its best this year, though the competition for that title is tougher. Out front is Tom Maguire, one of the most gracious hosts in town; out back now is Jason Bartley, who has an especially creative way with apparently everyday ingredients. Pricey, but you get what you pay for.

Paramount

New Art Gallery Building, Lorne St, Ph: 377 9973.

Website: www.paramountrestaurant.co.nz

By the time you get to 'two short blacks and the bill, please,' it's obvious that Emma and Trevor Griggs' fine dining room deserves its place at the top table of the city's restaurants. Trevor's modern take on traditional dishes produces one of the few menus where you run an eye down the courses and think, 'I'd be happy to eat anything here.'

Sails

Westhaven Drive, City, Ph: 378 9890.

Website: www.sailsrestaurant.co.nz

Twenty years of seafood and foreshore issues are celebrated at the Westhaven waterfront establishment. It's a class act from the management, front-of-house staff, sommeliers and especially chef Jason Blackie, who has an award-winning way with modern seafood dishes. We reckon you should go at lunchtime to enjoy the unparalleled feeling of eating on the deck of one of the yachts moored outside.

Soul
Viaduct Harbour,
Ph: 356 7249.
Website: www.soulsearch.co.nz

Night and day, you'll find
them, Auckland's young,
beautiful and Blahnik-heeled
at play. Soul's waterfront location is home to what Conde
Nast Traveler rates one of the
hottest new restaurants in the
world. Superb NZ cuisine,
tending towards seafood, by
Judith Tabron, queen of the
city's best kitchens, and her
young chef, Nick Huffman.

The French Café
210B Symonds St,
Ph: 377 1911.

Don't believe everything you
read: it's not French and it's
not a cafe. This elegant restaurant in a red-light area
above the city is a national
treasure that has been home
to some of New Zealand's
finest cooks for 18 years.
Chef-owner Simon Wright
and his wife, maitre d'
Creghan Molloy Wright, con-
tinue the commitment to the
best of classically influenced
food, wine, service and style.

Toto
53 Nelson St, Ph: 302 2665.

Love this room, whitewashed and heavy-beamed like an Italian farmhouse. Love the atmosphere, wafting in on clouds of olio and brunello from Italy, especially when a diner gets up from the table, drops his napkin and launches into an aria on Thursday's opera nights. The food blends traditional values, local ingredients and cosmopolitan ideas; the wine cellar is broad, deep and expensive.

White
Hilton Hotel, Princes Wharf, Ph: 978 2000.

Drool. First at the view from the prow of the Hilton, reaching into the harbour like an ocean liner, then at young Kiwi chef Geoff Scott's deceptively simple food, based on enhancing natural, clean flavours of the main ingredients with lighter style sauces, honed at La Gavroche in London and Hotel de Paris, Monte Carlo. Be warned, you'll pay for the privilege.

SOUTH, WEST, WAIHEKE

Bowmans

597 Mt Eden Rd, Mt Eden, Ph: 638 9676.

Website: www.bowmans.co.nz

A bistro of understated elegance that offers an outstanding selection of wines; a menu that matches every dish with an appropriate glass of wine; and superbly cooked food that's intelligent but doesn't shout 'look at me.'

Claret

127 Onehunga Mall, Onehunga, Ph: 622 2988.

Onehunga residents are lucky to have this buzzy café-restaurant close to home – and they know it, which can make it difficult for outsiders to find a table. The hosts lay on a warm and friendly greeting, chef Jack Peri offers interesting twists on bistro favourites, and it has the bonus of BYO. For those unused to this Kiwi custom, that means you can bring your own wine.

One Tree Grill

9 Pah Rd, Greenwoods Corner, Ph: 625 6407.

Website: www.onetreegrill.co.nz

Guy Malyon has created two of Auckland's best suburban restaurants in Halo and One Tree Grill (for visitors who don't get the joke, the neighbouring mountain is One Tree Hill, subject of the U2 song). Here, executive chef Simon Moss dreams up surprising combinations of flavours; his desserts are particular favourites. Each is matched to a wine, usually by the glass.

Palazzo Roma

31 Creek St, Drury,

Ph: 294 9004.

There may be more unlikely settings for a restaurant than an industrial estate on the outskirts of Drury, which is almost halfway down the motorway from the Skytower to Hamilton. Amid antique statues, outdoor furniture, bowers and leaves, superchefs Simon Gault (Gault@george) and Tony Astle (Antoine's) have installed Eugene Hamilton, formerly of Euro, and a contemporary Italian menu that is, as they like to say in the Michelin, worth the detour.

Point 5 Nine
5-9 Pt Chevalier Rd, Pt Chevalier, Ph: 815 9595.

Like Elvis says, don't be fooled. Behind the hard-to-find exterior on a surburban shopping square, you will find exciting, ingenious takes on classic dishes from the Med and Asia served in a stylish Pacific-themed room. The food is fresh, inspired, perfectly cooked, and is the star of an excellent, unpretentious restaurant that gets the wine, service and atmosphere spot on too.

The Hunting Lodge
Waimauku, Ph: 411 8259.

Recently facelifted (if that word can be applied to such a gracious old lady as this 130-year-old colonial cottage), take the 40-minute drive to the western countryside for hearty, traditional food, wine and service. Our tip: summer lunch on the verandah, overlooking gardens and vines.

Soljans Estate Cafe
366 State Highway 16, Kumeu, Ph: 412 5858.
Website: www.soljans.co.nz

Run by one of West Auckland's famous Dalmatian wine-growing families, the estate added a new wine cellar and café in 2002 and has barely had time to change the table-cloths since. Food ranges from French toast wrapped in bacon to delicately cooked mains such as fresh salmon poached in olive oil and sauvignon blanc. There's a kids' menu, too, with Kiwi delicacies like Vegemite sandwiches.

Te Whau Vineyard and Cafe
218 Te Whau Drive, Oneroa,
Waiheke Island, Ph: 372 7191.
Website: www.tewhau.co.nz

On a summer afternoon, after a 40-minute fast-ferry ride through the Hauraki Gulf to Waiheke and a meal atop the winery overlooking the vines and spectacular water and island views, you may understand why the New York Wine Spectator rates this 'one of the best restaurants in the world for wine lovers.'

Meals To Go

Sloppy burgers and soggy chips just don't cut it any more. These days we demand more of fast food: better variety, flavour and taste. Our panel of experts from *Viva* scoured Auckland to find the best of the best. We rated them on taste, speed of service, the menu variety and whether all of that made us want to go back for more. So here they are, *Viva*'s Ultimate Takeout Food Award winners for 2003. Bon appetit.

BEST OVERALL

Real
18 Anzac St, Takapuna, Ph: 488 7737.
Right from the word go Real has been a winner. For the health-conscious, it's a great find. They flame-grill their organic chicken using no oil or fat. There are salads that combine fantastic foods and flavours. Costs: $26.50 for two quarter chickens, two small salads and a serving of roast paprika potatoes.

RUNNER-UP and BEST ASIAN

East
171 Ponsonby Rd, Ponsonby, Ph: 360 6085.
It's hard to beat East if you're in the mood for a taste from the Orient. It offers modern Asian cuisine that's fast, economical and so, so good. Noodle and rice dishes are the house speciality, presented in cool white New York-style cardboard boxes. Costs: main dishes start at $10 and side

dishes (Thai fish cakes, dim sims etc) are all $3.50

Viva also recommends: Otto Woo, Ponsonby.

BEST THAI

Thai Isaan
136 Hinemoa St, Birkenhead, Ph: 480 0574.

Time and time and again people told us about their fantastic experiences at Thai Isaan. We can see why: great service and generous servings of the best Thai food in town. Everything is so good that it's hard to pick a favourite dish, but if we're forced to we'd recommend the prawn curry, grilled scallops with tamarind sauce and the stirfried chicken with honey, pineapple and cashew nuts. Costs: all mains come in under $20. Entrees average around $7. They have a 10 per cent discount on pick up, too.

Viva also recommends: Mekong Neua, Kingsland and Sawadee, Ponsonby

BEST PIZZA

Il Buco
113 Ponsonby Rd, Ponsonby, Ph: 360 4414.

This is about as good as pizza gets – traditional thin crust and heavenly toppings. Buy it by the slice and choose from around seven varieties which change each day. Warning: they're addictive.

Costs: At $3–$4 a pizza slice, it's terrific value.

Viva also recommends: One Red Dog, Takapuna, and SPQR, Ponsonby

BEST INDIAN

Oh Calcutta
149–155 Parnell Rd, Parnell, Ph: 377 9090.

If you wait for a quiet time to visit this place, you'll be waiting forever. The flow of people in the doors is relentless. There is a wide-ranging menu featuring dishes from northern and southern India, including old favourites such as butter chicken, lamb rogan josh and beef madras. The best curry in town - any way you like it.

Costs: main dishes range from $11.90 (vegetarian) to $19 (seafood and meat) and come with steamed rice. Naan and roti are between $2.75 and $3.95.

Viva also recommends: Shahi, Herne Bay, and Mithai, Birkenhead

BEST ITALIAN

Delicious
472 Richmond Rd, Grey Lynn, Ph: 360 7590.
Yes, they were winners in this category last year and we scoured Auckland to try to find better, really we did. But we can't go past Delicious with their classic flavour combinations, the wide variety of freshly made pasta and terrific prices. Oh, and don't even think about walking out the door before you've picked something out from the dessert cabinet which has a stunning selection of traditional Italian cakes.

Costs: all main dishes are between $14 and $15.50. Smaller servings are $8.50. Desserts are $6.

Viva also recommends: Gina's, City

BEST ON THE WEB (or BEST DELIVERY)

Gobble
Website: www.gobble.co.nz, Ph: 0800 846 2253.
No doubt you will have seen the scooters around town delivering gourmet takeout meals. The website is easy to follow and the range of meals is impressive, including a good variety of vegetarian dishes. The servings are quite generous

and extremely tasty. The only drawback is that Gobble delivers in Northcote, Takapuna, Auckland City and immediate inner-city suburbs only.

Costs: very reasonable. All mains are $12, salads and pizza (for one) are $9, gourmet sandwiches and melts are $8.

Viva also recommends: Urban Gourmet

BEST VARIETY

Zarbo
24 Morrow St, Newmarket, Ph: 520 2721.
For dedicated foodies, this is paradise. Zarbo recently launched its Zarbo2Go range, which changes daily.

If you can't make up your mind, ask the friendly staff to whip you a special picnic hamper with a selection of their goodies.

Costs: deli items start at $6.95 and Zarbo2Go meals start $12.95. Picnic hampers range from $16.50 to 29.95

Viva also recommends: Forbes for Food, Kohimarama, and Rocket Kitchen, Ponsonby

BEST VALUE

Fatimas
240 Ponsonby Rd, Ponsonby, Ph: 376 9303.
We just can't go past this place. Always good, always fresh, and crikey those potato kofta are good: mini croquettes of grated potato deep fried and served with garlic aoli.

Mediterranean cuisine is the feature here. It's no wonder that there's almost always a queue at this place - the food is good, fresh, and the menu is wide ranging.

Costs: at less than $20 for dinner for two, this is great value.

*full reviews on www.nzherald.co.nz/entertainment/restaurants

Vineyards

WEST AUCKLAND

KUMEU/HUAPAI VINEYARDS

Coopers Creek
State Highway 16, North of Huapai, Kumeu, Ph: 412 8560.
Open: Mon to Fri 9.30 am–5.30 pm Sat, Sun 10.30 am–5.30 pm.
Cellar sales, mail order, picnic area, barbecue facilities, small groups by appointment only. Free tastings up to 10 people, $3 per head over 10 people, slightly better prices than shops.

Matua Valley Wines
Waikoukou Valley Rd, Waimauku, Ph: 411 8301, Freephone: 0800 628 829.
Open: Mon to Fri 9 am–5 pm, Sat 10 am–6 pm (in summer), Sat 10 am–5 pm (in winter), Sun 11 am–4.30 pm all year round.
Cellar sales, mail order, tasting, picnic area, restaurant and groups by prior arrangements only, free tastings up to 10 people, over 10 people, cost per head by arrangement.

Nobilo Wine Group (includes Selaks label)
45 Station Rd, Huapai, Ph: 412 6666, Freephone: 0800 662 456.
Website: www.nobilo.co.nz
Open: Mon to Fri 9 am–5 pm, weekends & public holidays 10 am–5 pm.
Cellar sales, mail order, groups by arrangement, free tastings for groups of up to 10 people, above this number charge $2 per head, most wines 5 percent cheaper per case than shops.

Harrier Rise Vineyard
748 Waitakere Rd, PO Box 489, Kumeu, Ph: 412 7256.
Open: Sat & Sun 11 am–6 pm.
Cellar sales, tasting and mail orders, tastings $3 per head, usually cheaper than shop prices.

Kumeu River Wines Limited
550 Highway 16, Kumeu, Ph: 412 8415.
Open: Mon to Fri 9 am–5.30 pm, Sat 11 am–5 pm.
Cellar sales, mail order, tours and groups by appointment, tasting available but group tours by appointment $10 per head, not necessarily cheaper than shops.

HENDERSON VINEYARDS

Babich Wines Limited
Babich Rd, Henderson, Auckland, Ph: 833 7859.
Website: www.babichwines.co.nz
Open: Mon to Fri 9 am–5 pm, Sat 9 am–6 pm, Sun 11 am–5 pm.
Cellar sales, mail order, picnic areas, pétanque area, groups by appointment only.

Collards Winery
303 Lincoln Rd, Henderson, Ph: 838 8341.
Open: Mon to Sat 9 am–5 pm, Sun 11 am–5 pm.
Cellar sales, mail order, winery tours by special appointment June–Nov, free tastings regardless of the size of the group (bookings essential), 10 percent cheaper than shop prices.

Corbans Wines Limited
426–448 Great North Rd, Henderson, Ph: 837 3390.
Open: Mon to Sat, 9 am–6 pm.
Cellar sales, mail order, groups, free tastings for individuals, groups of 10 plus charge $2 per head, on average less than shop prices by 50 cents to $1, closed Sundays.

Lincoln Vineyards

130 Lincoln Rd, Henderson, Ph: 838 6944.

Open: Mon to Fri 9 am–5.30 pm, Sat & Sun 10 am–6 pm (in summer), Sat 10 am–5 pm, Sun 11 am–5 pm (in winter).

Cellar sales, mail order, tour and groups by arrangement, group tastings $3 per head, generally cheaper than shops, informal tastings in cellar at all times.

Pleasant Valley Wines

322 Henderson Valley Rd, Henderson, Ph: 838 8857.

Open: Mon to Sat 9 am–5.30 pm, Sun 11 am–5.30 pm.

Cellar sales, mail order, groups by prior arrangement, eating facilities, picnic area, Sat & Sun wine bar/café open from 11.30 am–4 pm with live music from Sept–June.

Soljans Estate Winery

366 State Highway 16, Kumeu, Ph: 412 5858, Freephone: 0508 SOLJAN.

Website: www.soljans.co.nz

Open: Mon to Sat 9 am–5.30 pm, Sun 11 am–5.30 pm.

Tastings complimentary unless in a group of 10, which is $3 per person, tours available, and a tour and tasting costs $5.50 per person, Sunday sales and tastings, generally cheaper than shop prices.

St Jerome Wines

219 Metcalfe Rd, Henderson, Ph: 833 6205.

Open: Mon to Sat 9 am–6 pm, Sun noon–5 pm.

Cellar sales, mail order, groups (up to 12 persons only).

West Brook Winery

215 Ararimu Valley Rd, Waimauku, Ph: 411 9924.

Open: Mon to Sat 10 am–5 pm, Sun 11 am–5 pm.

Cellar sales, mail order, group tasting by appointment and bookings essential, picnic area, groups of 8–10 plus charged $3 per person for tastings, $6 per person for cheese and crackers as well, they order in cheeses especially so booking is essential, generally cheaper than shop prices.

SOUTH AUCKLAND

Villa Maria Estate
5 Kirkbride Rd, Mangere, Ph: 255 0660.
Website: www.villamaria.co.nz
Open: 7 days 9 am–6 pm.

Cellar sales, mail order, tours by appointment, free tastings although for tours of 20 people plus cost of $5 per person, generally cheaper than shop prices.

WAIHEKE ISLAND VINEYARDS

For a full listing of the Waiheke Island vineyards, see 'Island-hopping', p. 49.

Nightclubs, Bars & Pubs

Auckland bar-life remains pleasantly sedate early in the week, although most places will stay open until after midnight if the demand is there, but expect a thriving scene on Thursdays, as the club-going crowd make a head-start on the weekend. On Fridays and Saturdays, the most popular bars will be jumping until close (any time between midnight and 3 am depending on their individual liquor licence).

We can't list them all but we've chosen establishments to suit a variety of tastes.

For live music gigs at bars & pubs, visit our website www.nzherald.co.nz/entertainment/whatsonthisweek/ or read TimeOut in the *Weekend Herald*. For reviews of pubs and bars, check out *Barfly* each Wednesday in the *New Zealand Herald*'s *Viva* section.

CITY BARS

Atrium Bar
Level 2, Sky City, Cnr Victoria and Federal Sts, Ph: 912 6000.

Located a dice's throw from the main gaming room at Sky City, the Atrium Bar is a mild-mannered rest area by day, then loosens up to party mode at night – especially in the weekends.

Classic Comedy & Bar
321 Queen St, Ph: 373 4321.
www.comedy.co.nz for gig guide

Pure comedy and the stomping ground for established and up'n'coming local comedians and the occasional international guest. It's overwhelmingly busy if a noted comedian is starring, but is otherwise attractive as a location for a mid-week nightcap.

Corner Bar
Cnr Shortland and High Sts, Ph: 302 0747.

Small, cosy bar in the old De Bretts Hotel. It has been through several identity crises since the '80s and it is once again popular. An ideal place for an after-work drink or a cocktail before heading off for bright lights elsewhere.

Crow Bar
26 Wyndham St, Ph: 366 0398.

A late-night drinking venue, situated underground in the heart of the central city. The bar staff are exceptionally professional and make a fine cocktail. In the weekend wee hours, Crow Bar can buzz with the city's beautiful people, or try it mid-week for a more mellow tipple.

Deschlers
17 High St, Ph: 379 6811.

Jazz fans queue here. A respected stalwart of the local bar scene, Deschlers, a cruisy 1950s-style jazz lounge, delivers live music three nights a week (Mon, Wed, Sat) and offers Soul sounds such as Aretha Franklin, Otis Redding and Barry White for the remainder.

Dispensary
Cnr Hobson and Victoria Sts, Ph: 309 2118.

One of the few bars in Auckland open 24 hours. It attracts a lot of hospitality staff winding down after a long shift at other bars, restaurants and clubs around town, and with Sky City just across the road, late night and early morning casino-fiends. This actually was the site of a chemist. These days it dispenses standard pub-style drinks.

Elbow Room

12 Durham Lane East, Ph: 377 0301.

Once known as DLAF (Drink Like a Fish) and Bar Durham in previous lives, this is a small, square, intimate bar – the kind of place where everybody knows or will know your name. Conversations here are not held in private so expect to swap views with loyal regulars and bar staff.

Green Room

Shed 22, Princes Wharf, Viaduct, Ph: 362 0776.

Subtle and stylish, it's a small but perfectly formed oceanside bolt hole. There's plenty of champagne, beer, spirits and an array of Martinis to choose from; the utterly delightful and original Joan Crawford and Clark Gable concoctions come highly recommended.

Luminaire

6 Beresford St, off Karangahape Rd, Ph: 308 9090.

White interiors and cool blue lighting – the place is perfectly appointed for sipping on a vodka or two. The bar continues to specialise in the Russian drink, offering more than 40 varieties for connoisseurs to taste.

Match

Cnr Pitt and Hopetoun Sts, Ph: (09) 378 0440.

Sophisticated and stylish appealing to an urban and well-heeled crowd. Here you are waited on. It's a cocktail heaven and to have a simple vodka, lemon and lime is to waste the talents of the bartender.

Mexican Café & Bar

67 Victoria St West, Ph: 373 2311.

Their margaritas are said to be the best in town. During happy hour from 5–7pm every day, you can have them shaken or frozen, fruit flavoured or original. Aucklanders have a soft spot for this place. It's lively and colourful – and turns 21 this year [2004].

Mo's

Cnr Federal and Wolfe Sts, Ph: 366 6066.

Hidden away in a nondescript corner of the city, its maximum intake would number less than 30. When it's busy, a bubbly, friendly atmosphere prevails and, as with The Elbow Room, your business won't remain your business for long. Ideal for post-work or pre-dinner drinks.

O'Carrolls Bar
10 Vulcan Lane, Ph: 300 7117.

Cosy Irish bar next door to the Belgian Beer Café. There's a good feeling to O'Carrolls and there could be a bit of an Irish singalong if the crowd gets merry enough. Guinness and Kilkenny are obviously house favourites but the bar staff can whip up anything you fancy.

Pickle
2 Hobson St, City, Ph: (09) 307 7030.

The Hobson Street Lounge was the scene of many a late-night cocktail. Refurbished and renamed as Pickle, it still produces the same high standard of cocktails including the HSL's apple martini.

Rakinos
1st Floor, 35 High St (opp Freyberg Square), Ph: 358 3535.

Through the day it has a relaxed café atmosphere. At night, a popular bar and a venue for live music. Sunday nights has live jazz and jam sessions, which feature some of the best Auckland has to offer in jazz musicians.

Stark's Café & Champagne Bar
Cnr Wellesley and Queen Sts, Ph 377 0277.

The street-level café and bar attached to the Civic is named in tribute to dancer Freda Stark, who wowed the American Troops at the theatre in the 1940s. It operates as a café during the day and then turns into a bar with a wide wine and cocktail list and around 18 varieties of champagne to tickle your nose.

Supper Club
2 Beresford St, City, Ph: 300 5040.

Just off Karangahape Rd, it is located in renovated public toilets and transit station from the 1930s. Nice spot to sup a drink while watching the sun go down or ideal late-night (and early morning) hangout for those who are carrying on the party from K' Rd's clubland.

Tabac
6 Mills Lane, Ph: 366 6067.

There's a sophisticated yet amiable vibe early in the evening that builds to a small rumble as the night wears on. A popular after-work spot with young white-collar cellular-phone owners, Tabac also offers a private, more peaceful bar, the Velvet Room, for members and VIP guests.

Wine Loft
67 Shortland St, Ph: 379 5070.

Located upstairs, it has an intimate and sophisticated appeal. Customers tend to be mainly business people and wine is their obvious choice. You'll find Australian and New Zealand vintages alongside bottles from Spain, Argentina, France and Italy.

HERNE BAY/ PONSONBY BARS

Elbow Room
198 Jervois Rd, Herne Bay, Ph: 376 2613.

It boasts an impressive selection of wine and champagne, with Heineken the beer of choice. On slower evenings the discreet big screen TV is continuously tuned to sports, although regular patrons (age range 25–50 yrs) keep Elbow humming with conversation on the weekends.

Garage Bar
152 Ponsonby Rd, Ph: 378 8237.

Quieter mid-week, Garage is packed and pumping on Fridays and Saturdays, with resident and guest DJs playing on site. Courteous and easygoing bar staff matched with a party-minded clientele ensure Garage is a lively place to drink.

Lime
167 Ponsonby Rd, Ph: 360 7167. Closed Sundays.

Size doesn't matter at Lime, a narrow, low-ceiling drinking den safely tucked away on Ponsonby Rd. There's little or no room for fittings or furniture – more than 30 patrons would prove a tight squeeze. Expect Tom Jones and Kenny Rogers on the stereo.

Safari Lounge
116 Ponsonby Rd, Ph: 378 7707.

An ideal spot for daytime drinking when the sun is out, the tavern-sized Safari Lounge features a spacious courtyard outside, pool tables, booths and couches inside. It spotlights local DJ talent to a 20 to 30-something crowd six nights a week.

Surrender Dorothy
3/175 Ponsonby Rd, Ph: 376 4460.

Named after Dorothy from *The Wizard of Oz*, the bar opened nearly a decade ago catering mostly for a young, glamorous, mainly gay clientele. Today all are welcome, regardless of sexual preference. Most of the clientele are regulars and this gives it an extra friendly atmosphere, as people greet and wave at one another. Theatrical and fun.

CITY PUBS

Civic Tavern
Cnr of Queen and Wellesley Sts, Auckland Central, Ph: 373 3684.

The Civic Tavern houses an Irish bar and a London bar, a good mix of New Zealand beers and, they say, 100 beers from around the world to cater to many tastes. Solid Jazz Thursday to Saturday nights from local bands and artists.

King's Arms Tavern
59 France St, Newton, Ph: 373 3240.

It's the music that really makes this pub worth a visit. Long-established inner city pub in danger of dying out resurrects itself as a regular venue for loud, rocking young New Zealand bands (Wed to Sat).

Loaded Hog
204 Quay St, Viaduct Basin, Ph: 366 6491.

Prime position for viewing comings-and-goings at the Viaduct Basin. It has an outside drinking and eating area, roomy bar, rowdy atmosphere in the evenings. Light meals and bar snacks available. Wine by the glass too, or try their medal-winning beers Hog Gold or Red Dog Draught.

Muddy Farmer
13 Wyndham St, Ph: 336 1265.

Irish to the Corr, it's a haunt for beer and Guinness lovers and as you might presume, celebrates St Patrick's Day in fine style. It's nestled in the Heritage complex (old Farmers building) and has its street level entrance opposite the car park.

Occidental Belgian Beer Café
6–8 Vulcan Lane, Auckland Central, Ph: 300 6226.

The old Occidental was once a typical New Zealand public bar, home to a hard-drinking crowd, but it has style in its new guise as a spacious, dark-wood pub with classic Belgian beers on tap. A local touch of class comes from an extensive menu of Kiwi mussel dishes in pots (small) or filling platters (large), in many disguises.

Playhouse Pub
Force Entertainment Centre, Queen St, Ph: 979 2470.

Located in the same building as the cinema complex, it offers a stunning view of the Aotea Centre aka The Edge and the Aotea Square. The crowd changes depending on what's on close by. Bodington's on tap, as well as the usual assortment of beers, wines and spirits. English pub-style meals are also served.

Queens Head Tavern
396 Queen St, Ph: 302 0223.

It looks like a typical English pub and here you can step back in time and space, indulge in a ham steak with pineapple, a lager and a game of pool, or watch the latest sporting match on one of the many televisions on the walls. All the usual spirits and a decent selection of beer. A mainly older and middle of the road crowd mixed with tourists from nearby hotels.

Shakespeare Tavern and Brewery
61 Albert St, Auckland Central, Ph: 373 5396.

One of the first micro-breweries in town, this pub has modern technology and old-style pub atmosphere in equal measures. Award-winning beers include Pompey Bums Rumpty Ale, Falstaff's Real Ale, Shylock's Light Ale and Puck's Fundamental.

SUBURBAN PUBS

De Post Belgian Beer Café
466 Mt Eden Rd (in Mt Eden Village opposite Ngauruhoe St), Ph: 630 9330.

Once the site of the Mt Eden Post Office, the two-storied building with upstairs balcony is a pub offering locals the beers and menu of its popular, city sister.

The Gables
Cnr of Jervois Rd and Kelmarna Ave, Herne Bay, Ph: 376 4994.

Jazz (Wed), sport and trivial pursuit quizzes run through this friendly neighbourhood pub's week. Favourite spot for watching sports games on the big TV. Guinness on tap, pub meals and bar snacks.

Galbraith's Ale House
2 Mt Eden Rd (Symonds St end), Ph: 379 3557.

From its classy micro-brewery visible in a large room beside the bar, this pub serves its own beers rich with character from the tap, as well as many English beers. They stock a good range of single malt whiskies.

Horse and Trap
3 Enfield St, Mt Eden, Ph: 630 3055, or 630 1977.

In a heritage building, this tavern goes for a rustic Kiwi style. There's a particular emphasis on NZ beers, especially Monteith's range associated with the West Coast of the South Island, and a New Zealand wild food theme. Bars are split between stand-up – with a sports emphasis, and sit-down casual. Lunchtime Jazz on Sundays.

Masonic Tavern
29 King Edward Pde, Devonport, Ph: 445 0485.

A short ferry-ride across the harbour and a pleasant 500 m harbourside stroll will bring you to the olde-world Masonic on the Devonport waterfront. Wide-window views of the harbour and passing yachts. Ideal on a summer's day.

NIGHTCLUBS

Deregulation of the liquor industry in the early nineties resulted in a blurring of the lines between bars and clubs. With many bars having longer opening hours and featuring a DJ and dance floor (the traditional domain of nightclubs), clubs have had to adapt to a changing market. As in most cosmopolitan cities around the world, 'club culture' has introduced itself into the Auckland lifestyle, and every other weekend it seems an international DJ is playing somewhere. Top DJs from London, Detroit and Paris play here regularly (for gigs, TimeOut, *Weekend Herald* or visit www.nzherald.co.nz/entertainment/whatsonthisweek/). Local live music is featuring more and international groups perform here regularly.

As a general rule, smart attire and a positive demeanour will ensure your access to most clubs.

Bass
10 Victoria St, Auckland Central, Ph: 379 7897.

Below ground on Victoria Street, Bass is a nightclub strictly for fans of Hip-hop and American R&B, complete with a medium-sized dance floor and pool tables. With resident DJs playing every weekend, a regular, mostly Polynesian, crowd arrives early and stays late.

Centro Club and Lounge
Level 1, 26 Wyndham St, Auckland Central, Ph: 377 3225.

Dark, stylish atmosphere, lots of seating, lounge area with leather booths, long bar, separate dance floor, international DJs and weekly events.

Coast
Level 7, Hewlett and Packard Building, Princess Wharf, Waterfront, Ph: 300 9966.

Sophisticated House music and general surrounds oozing style and pretension. Great harbour views and huge space.

Fu Bar
166 Queen St, Auckland Central, Ph: 309 3079.

Drum 'n' bass, hip-hop and two-step feature on different nights, and sometimes leading and international turntablists. Dark and underground in atmosphere and music style.

Galatos

17 Galatos St, parallel to K'Rd, Ph: 303 1928.

Housing three levels, Galatos offers something for all tastes. The lounge upstairs is host to funk and soul DJs as well as live bands while two floors below in the basement drum and bass and hip-hop play to the early hours of the morning. The main stage is host to both local and occasionally international live acts.

Khuja Lounge

536 Queen St, cnr Queen St & K'Rd, Ph: 377 3711.

It's worth climbing the four flights of stairs to one of the coolest clubs in Auckland with DJs and live percussion from Wednesday to Sunday. The ambience is dark and exotic like the music, making the club a regular venue for soul, funk and other urban live acts.

420

Upstairs, 373 Karangahape Rd, City, Ph: 021 597 876.

Website: www.420.co.nz

One of the best places for hip-hop and R & B of the kind that is played on MaiFM. Excellent combination of bar and nightclub that's friendly and lively but with a sophisticated touch. The dance floor is big enough for a good-sized crowd. Open Thursday to Saturday from 9 pm until late.

20 Top Attractions

Tour buses will inevitably include most of the 'must see' attractions in Auckland such as the Auckland War Memorial Museum, Kelly Tarlton's Antarctic Encounter and Underwater World, the Auckland Zoo and a drive to the top of Mt Eden. But with a bit of extra knowledge, you can take your time, and enjoy what you want without following the crowd. We've grouped our top attractions by area so that you can see what else is close by.

Auckland War Memorial Museu

Activities and Attractions

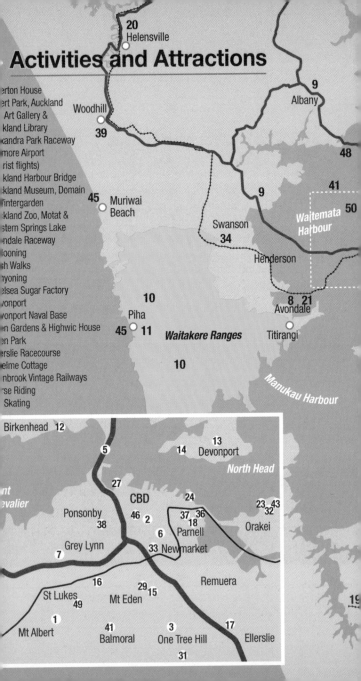

20 Helensville

9 Albany

Woodhill **39**

48

41

45 Muriwai Beach

50 Waitemata Harbour

Swanson **34**

Henderson

erton House
ert Park, Auckland
Art Gallery &
kland Library
xandra Park Raceway
more Airport
rist flights)
kland Harbour Bridge
kland Museum, Domain
intergarden
kland Zoo, Motat &
stern Springs Lake
ndale Raceway
looning
sh Walks
nyoning
elsea Sugar Factory
vonport
vonport Naval Base
n Gardens & Highwic House
n Park
erslie Racecourse
elme Cottage
nbrook Vintage Railways
rse Riding
Skating

10 Piha

45 **11**

Waitakere Ranges

10

9

8 **21**
Avondale

Titirangi

Manukau Harbour

Birkenhead **12**

5

13 Devonport
14

North Head

27

CBD

24

23 **43**
32

Ponsonby
38

46 **2**

37 **36**
18
Parnell

Orakei

nt
evalier

Grey Lynn

6

33 Newmarket

7

16

29 **15**

Remuera

St Lukes
49

1

Mt Eden

41
Balmoral

3
One Tree Hill

17
Ellerslie

Mt Albert

31

19

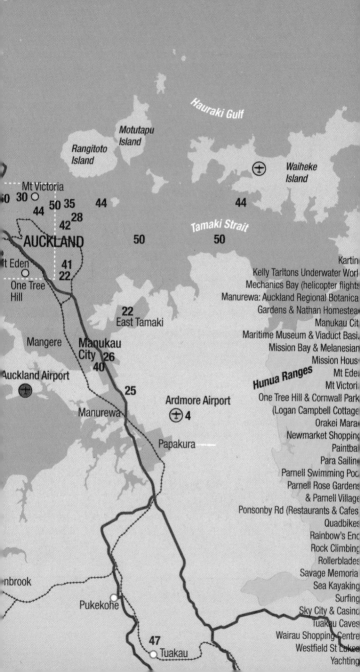

Haural Gulf

Motutapu
Island

Rangitoto
Island

Waiheke
Island

Mt Victoria
30
50 35   44
44   50
42 28
AUCKLAND   50

Tamaki Strait

44

50   50

Mt Eden   Kartin
41   Kelly Tarltons Underwater Worl
22   Mechanics Bay (helicopter flights
One Tree   Manurewa: Auckland Regional Botanica
Hill   Gardens & Nathan Homestea
22   Manukau Cit
East Tamaki   Maritime Museum & Viaduct Basi
Mission Bay & Melanesian
Mission Hous
Mangere   Manukau   Hunua Ranges   Mt Ede
City   26   Mt Victori
40   One Tree Hill & Cornwall Park
Auckland Airport   (Logan Campbell Cottage
25   Orakei Mara
Manurewa   Ardmore Airport   Newmarket Shopping
4   Paintba
Papakura   Para Sailin
Parnell Swimming Poo
Parnell Rose Gardens
& Parnell Village
Ponsonby Rd (Restaurants & Cafes
Quadbikes
Rainbow's End
Rock Climbing
Rollerblades
nbrook   Savage Memoria
Sea Kayaking
Pukekohe   Surfing
Sky City & Casino
Tuakau Caves
47   Wairau Shopping Centre
Tuakau   Westfield St Lukes
Yachting

Kelly Tarlton's Antarctic Encounter and Underwater World.

Auckland Zoo.

CITY

SKY TOWER

Sky City, Cnr Victoria and Federal Sts, Ph: 912 6000 or freephone 0800 759 2489.
It has the undisputed top view in the city and ideal to visit
first. The 360° round view highlights the isthmus of Auckland
on one side, and on the other, the islands of the Hauraki
Gulf stretch to the horizon. Alternatively, take in the view
from the restaurant, which takes one hour to revolve the full
360°, and around the 80 km distant view. Watch out for
harnessed jumpers (see Sky Tower Jump, page 36).

Sky City also contains the Sky City Casino. Open 24 hours,
7 days, free entry, patrons must be 20 years or older. Neat
and tidy standard of dress required.

Restaurants and entertainment in the bars, and at the
attached Sky City theatre there are concerts, musicals, plays
and films.

Sky Tower opens daily from 8.30 am until late. Adults
$15, Senior citizens $13.50, children $7.50 (5–14 yrs),
under 5 free. $3 extra for top level platform 'Skydeck'.
Backpacker, YHA concessions and family passes available.

VIADUCT

Entrances from Customs St West, Fanshawe St, Lower Hobson St, Quay St.
It's an easy walk from the Sky Tower down Hobson St or Albert
St to the Viaduct Harbour. Developed as a 'village' specifically
for the (successful) New Zealand defence of the America's
Cup trophy in 1999–2000, the multi-million dollar Viaduct
Harbour development is surrounded by restaurants bars,
cafés, apartments blocks and offices. It's a great place to
wander – especially on a sunny day and when superyachts
are moored. Concerts and entertainment abound during
summer; wining and dining are the thing. View the Maori
sculptures along the walkway, visit the New Zealand National

Maritime Museum and stroll nearby Princes Wharf for more restaurants, cafes and bars.

NEW ZEALAND NATIONAL MARITIME MUSEUM

Quay St, Auckland, Ph: 373 0800.

Auckland is known as the City of Sails, and the Maritime Museum on the harbour's edge is our celebration of sun and sea. It holds New Zealand's Maori, Polynesian and European maritime history, from the first journeys of the Maori to our shores to the English immigrants of the turn of the 19th century. Actors tell you the story, there's maritime art, the history of the America's Cup, and the chance to ride in one of the museum's boats, moored outside.

Open: daily (except Christmas day) 9am–5pm. Costs adults $12, concessions $6, family pass $28. Heritage Harbour Cruises: adults $15, concessions $7. Museum combo (includes cruise): adults $19, concessions $12.

CITY FRINGE

AUCKLAND WAR MEMORIAL MUSEUM

Auckland Domain, Domain Dr, Ph: 306 7067.
Website: www.akmuseum.org.nz

Built in 1929 as a memorial to the many New Zealanders who lost their lives in World War I, World War II and other conflicts abroad, the museum proudly boasts of having the world's leading collection of Maori treasures ('taonga' in Maori).

It has frequent changing exhibitions and recently created a stunning show to celebrate the 50th anniversary of Sir Edmund Hillary's ascent of Mt Everest (the exhibition is now travelling overseas).

The resident Manaia Maori cultural performance consists of a welcome, poi dance, stick game, weaponry display (the

fiercely whirled spear taiaha) and a haka – the war dance most popularly associated with the beginning of rugby games.

There are other special exhibitions to enjoy – fossils, bird song, porcelain, furniture, war memorabilia (including real aeroplanes), a forest recreated, an aquarium in miniature, insects, musical instruments, photographs, an historic city street, the moving war memorial roll of honour, and two children's interactive Discovery Centres, among the many other attractions.

Open: 7 days, 10 am–5 pm (except Christmas day, Anzac Day morning, April 25).

Costs: adults donation requested ($5 suggested), children free.

THE DOMAIN AND WINTERGARDENS

Once known as Pukekaroa, the 75 ha area of the Domain is one of Auckland's oldest parks and was created around the cone of an extinct volcano. It formed a natural amphitheatre which is now well-used sports fields and the site of hugely-popular outdoor concerts during the summer season.

There are also classic gardens, a duck pond fed by a natural spring, century-old trees and significant statues.

Just up the slope from the duck pond and Kiosk (created for the Great Industrial Exhibiton of 1913 and now the site for refreshments) lies the Wintergardens where something is always blooming. The Wintergardens are open all year round and entry is free.

PARNELL VILLAGE

Parnell Rd.

Next door to the Domain is a charming area that is the site of some of our oldest buildings. Auckland property visionary Les Harvey bought a run-down group of wooden Victorian villas in Parnell in the late 1960s and early 1970s. He

wanted to save a style of living for the community, and against the rules he restored finials, towers, bay windows and brick courtyards around the area, persuaded friendly shop owners to move their businesses there, and even fought the restrictive no-Saturday/Sunday trading laws then in place. Food, fashion, craft, art, design – all are represented in Parnell.

KELLY TARLTON'S UNDERWATER WORLD

23 Tamaki Dr, Ph: 528 0603 or 0800 805 050.
Website: www.new-zealand.com/KellyTarltons

Giant stingrays flap slowly through the water, sharks drift past and giant moray eels lurk in the one million litres of crystal-clear water in this distinctive aquarium-cum-underseas-adventure, which has been voted New Zealand's best visitor attraction.

The late Kelly Tarlton and his team converted large underground holding tanks (once used to discharge sewage waste into the harbour) to transform a dream into reality.

The Antarctic experience includes a ride in a heated Snow Cat (air temperature outside is minus 2–0°C) through a duplicated Antarctic landscape where you can see King Penguins living in freshly made snow and view them through underwater glass as they dive and swim. The whole visit normally takes about 45 minutes.

Open: 7 days, Summer (1 Dec to 28 Feb) 9 am–8 pm, and Winter (1 Mar to 30 Nov) 9 am–6 pm, Christmas day 10 am–5 pm. Shark feeding Tues and Thurs at 2 pm.

Costs: adults $25, children (5–14 yrs) $10 (4 yrs) $6, concessions and family passes available.

TAMAKI DRIVE

We featured this length of road in our Top Views and we mention it here for some of the other points of interest along its way.

From the city end on the harbour side is the container terminal Ferguson Wharf and Mechanics Bay, the base of the Auckland Rescue Helicopters.

Just up the rise on the right is Gladstone Rd, which leads to the clifftop Dove-Myer Robinson Park and the Parnell Rose Gardens, overlooking the inlet of Judges Bay, the historic St Stephen's Anglican Church and the recently refurbished Parnell Baths.

Tamaki Drive passes over Hobson Bay (old boat sheds on the right) and leads around to Okahu Bay, often the departure point for the striking waka (canoe) of local Maori tribe, Ngati Whatua. In summer, it is often seen out on the water or resting on the sand.

The entrance to the Michael Savage Memorial, a panoramic park named in honour of the first Labour Prime Minister of New Zealand and the founder of the Welfare State, is just around the corner. It lies adjacent to Takaparawha Regional Park and the Orakei Marae.

The Tamaki Yacht Club building, available for private functions, has a prime spot on the rocks before Tamaki Beach.

Tamaki Drive then winds through Mission Bay and its reserve. Popular all year round for its cafes, it is nearly standing room only during summer weekends as people throng to enjoy safe swimming at the beach, picnic in the adjacent park and play near the fountain area and the historic Melanesian Mission House.

If Mission Bay gets too crowded, there are always the next beaches – Kohimarama Beach and St Heliers Bay.

WESTERN SPRINGS

AUCKLAND ZOO

Motions Rd, Western Springs, Ph: 360 3819.
Website: www.aucklandzoo.co.nz

Auckland Zoo opened in 1922, but the animal-friendly modern version is a world away from the cages and concrete enclosures thought adequate then. Now there's a new home for sealions, a natural rainforest enclosure for the smaller monkeys which you can walk through, an aviary which puts you and the birds in the middle of some New Zealand bush, an elephant enclosure with hot showers, pools, elephant-sized toys and room for the elephants to exercise, a grasslands environment for the lions with interconnected habitats where African animals are able to roam together, and a habitat where giraffes and zebras share their waterholes, as in the wild. Among the 150 species and 500 animals in the zoo, the toy-like red pandas are a favourite, as is the kiwi house. This nocturnal setting for the night-dwelling kiwi means you have to let your eyes get accustomed to the low light before quietly observing New Zealand's famous flightless bird.

Take the Western Springs exit off the Northwestern Motorway. For bus information and timetables, phone Rideline on Ph: 306 6400. Free parking.

Open: 7 days (excluding Christmas day) 9.30 am–5.30 pm.

Costs: adults $13, senior citizens $9, students $10, children (4–15 yrs) $7 (under 4) free, family concessions available. During summer, the Explorer Bus provides a satellite service from the Auckland Museum hourly between 10.30 am–3.30 pm.

MOTAT AND SIR KEITH PARK MEMORIAL AVIATION COLLECTION

The Museum of Transport, Technology and Social History (MOTAT)
Great North Rd, Western Springs, Ph: 846 0199.

Volunteers gallantly maintain this preserve of old buses, planes, trains, trams, machinery, communications equipment, colonial shops and aviation memorabilia. Best bits for kids: getting into the cab of the 90-tonne K900 steam train, travelling on the tram, playing in the Science and Technology Centre. The Pioneer Aviators pavilion is almost a shrine to NZ's glamorous pioneer flier Jean Batten, but there are replicas of two Richard Pearse wired-together planes (more than a few New Zealanders claim the early 20th-century South Island aviator flew before the Wright brothers). At the airfield a tram ride away, check out the complete Solent flying boat Aranui in service from 1949–1960.

Open: 7 days (except Christmas day), 10 am–5 pm.

Costs: adults $10, children (5–16 yrs) $5, senior citizens $5.

WESTERN SPRINGS LAKE

Great North Rd, Western Springs.

The lake was one of Auckland's early water supplies and today the natural spring-fed lake harbours a variety of wildlife – swans, ducks, geese, pukeko and a growing number of native eel. A series of solid paths surround the lake, making this a relaxing and pleasant stop-off between the Auckland Zoo and Motat.

SOUTH AUCKLAND

RAINBOW'S END

Cnr Great South & Wiri Station Rds, Manukau City, Infoline Ph: 262 2044.
Website: www.rainbowsend.co.nz

Take a ride on the Fear Fall – Rainbows End's newest attraction. Two cars of four people seated on a controlled

ascent to the top of the tower, a pause – and then a drop at 80 kmph. Plus, the enchanted forest log flume, one of the most popular rides, with the watery twists and turns leading to a big plunge at the end. Here resides New Zealand's only Double Corkscrew roller coaster, and a goldrush ride in karts through an 'abandoned gold mine'. Also: bumper boats, dodgems, family karts (closed when raining), mini golf, 3D cinema with 180° curved screen, Cadbury Land Castle for under-10s. Some height restrictions apply to certain rides. Rides operate non-stop Sat/Sun/public and school holidays, and on a timetable at other times.

Open: 7 days, 10 am–5 pm (closed Christmas day), Dec 26 to Jan 9,10 am–8 pm.

Super Pass Costs (entry & unlimited rides for the whole day): adults (14 yrs & over) $35, children (4–13 yrs) $25, (2–3 yrs) $10, and 2 yrs and under free. Family group discounts available.

AUCKLAND REGIONAL BOTANIC GARDENS

Hill Rd, Manurewa, Ph: 267 1457.

A delightful park comprising 65 hectares of special plant collections and native forest in the midst of one of the fast-growing urban areas of Auckland, and now host to the annual Ellerslie Flower Show. The garden has over 10,000 plant types, from New Zealand natives to exotics, from all over the world (including a large area devoted to roses that attract thousands of visitors each spring and summer).

It's a 20-minute drive on the Southern Motorway from the city centre. Take the Manurewa off-ramp and turn left into Hill Rd.

HOWICK HISTORICAL VILLAGE

Bell's Rd, Lloyd Elsmore Park, Pakuranga, Ph: 576 9506.
Website: www.fencible.org.nz

In this recreated village of settlers' 'fencible' cottages, there are vivid scenes of life in colonial New Zealand and even more lively stories. There's a schoolroom of the time, a courthouse, and items of daily life – a baby's cradle suspended from the roof, a pig-scalding trough.

Costs: adults $10, children $5, senior citizens $8, family (2 adults & 2 children) $25.

WARBIRDS-DAKOTA

Ardmore Airport, Airfield Rd, Ardmore, Ph: 479 1378.

If scenic flight is your fancy, the New Zealand Warbirds Association offers something different. Every Sunday (weather permitting) it fires up the engines of its 60-year-old Dakota (or DC3) and takes passengers for sedate 30-minute cruises over Auckland. It swings past all the landmarks – Rangitoto Island, the Harbour Bridge, Sky Tower, Mt Eden, One Tree Hill.

Bookings are essential. Costs: adults $65, children (3–14 yrs) $40. Concessions: adult and child $100, over 60 yrs $60, 6 adults $360. Devonshire teas are available 30 minutes before departure.

GLENBROOK VINTAGE RAILWAYS

Glenbrook Station, Ph: 236 3546.

Puffing Billy and Thomas The Tank Engine fans queue here. Train enthusiasts started building the vintage railways along unused track in 1970, and today those volunteers operate a fully self-supporting steam railway from the Glenbrook Station, allowing visitors to experience travel from a bygone era.

Trains run on the hour from 11 am–4 pm on Sundays and most public holiday weekends from Labour Weekend

(October 26) until Queens Birthday Weekend (early June).

Fares: adults $12, children (aged 5–15 yrs) $6, family (2 adults and up to 6 school age children) $30.

The Farm Park is next door. Children find this particularly exciting in spring and early summer with the birth of new baby animals.

WEST AUCKLAND

MURIWAI BEACH AND GANNET COLONY
Muriwai Beach, ParksLine, Ph: 303 1530.

Remarkable by any standards, the Muriwai gannet colony is the sort of slightly spooky place that leaves people awestruck without quite knowing why. These enormous birds come here to breed from about October through to February before migrating to Australia. Jammed together on a giant rock, whose base is lashed by waves, they are best seen in windy conditions when their flights are at their most impressive. The colony is strictly protected but the opportunities for photography are spectacular.

Kids'/Family Fun

For family outings, especially with children under 12, the spread of activity around Auckland is as engaging and as high-energy as you want to make it, and is often packaged with fun for the adults, too.

Many of Auckland's top attractions will fascinate the kids – Kelly Tarlton's Antarctic Encounter and Underwater World, the view from the top of the Sky Tower – although be aware that these can all be quite costly for the whole family. The Auckland Museum, with its interactive Discovery Centres, is hard to beat. Auckland Zoo never fails to beguile the young, and the unpredictable animals are now more visible in their renovated eco-friendly enclosures – see the sea-lions through underwater viewing glass, pop your head up into the small plastic viewing bubbles in the middle of the meerkat enclosure, and talk to the small squirrel monkeys and cotton top tamarins swinging freely through the rain forest enclosure. See '20 Top Attractions', p. 105 for further information about these fun places to visit.

MUSEUMS

The National Maritime Museum has plenty of walk-in action (a ship's hold, sailing ship cabins) and boating fun outside if you want a brief harbour cruise. At the Museum of Transport, Technology and Social History (MOTAT) in Western Springs, the Science and Technology Centre lets the young create their own electricity with the plasma globe, bang on

musical pipes, sit in a moving earthquake café, draw star patterns, reflect in funny mirrors and ride in a tram (they're history here, although civilised cities such as Melbourne and Amsterdam have living originals).

PLAYGROUNDS

Numerous safe climbing, tunnelling, swinging constructions just for kids can be found at parks throughout Auckland. Some recommended playgrounds are:

Myers Park, just off Queen St, Auckland Central.

Victoria Park, Victoria St West, opposite Victoria Park Market.

Gladstone Park, Gladstone Rd (opposite the Rose Gardens in Parnell).

Mt Eden Park, at the base of the mountain on Mt Eden Rd.

Potter's Park, Cnr of Dominion & Balmoral Rds, Balmoral.

Cornwall Park, edge of the huge park centred on One Tree Hill (Manukau Rd entrance).

Grey Lynn Park, off Williamson Ave (shallow outdoor swimming pool in summer).

Western Park (bottom entrance, Beresford St).

Rocket Park, Wairere Ave, Mt Albert.

Mission Bay (playground on the grass is next to a café for weary, watching parents).

Western Springs, near the Zoo entrance (bonus: nearby lake with swans, geese and ducks to feed).

Devonport Reserve, King Edward Pde.

INDOOR PLAY ZONES

In recent times a number of indoor, supervised playing areas have cropped up that charge an entry fee for children (adults are free). Expansive areas, the latest in playing equipment, climbing frames, bouncy castles and other essential magnets for energetic children are available at these fun zones. Coffee and muffin areas are provided for watching adults.

Lollipops Playland
Ellerslie Racecourse, Morrin St, Ellerslie, Ph: 525 2950.
129 Onewa Rd, Birkenhead, Ph: 480 1166.
1a Rankin Ave, New Lynn, Ph: 827 5796.
Website: www.lollipops.co.nz

Kids 'n Action
Croftfield Lane (off Link Dr), Glenfield, Ph: 444 3366.

Chipmunks Children's Adventure Playgrounds
30 Downing St, Glenfield, Ph: 444 8766. Open: 7 days 9.30 am–6 pm.
201 Lincoln Rd, Henderson, Ph: 838 2033. Open: 7 days 9.30 am–6 pm.
6B Carr Rd, Mt Roskill, Ph: 624 4345. Open: 7 days 9.30 am–6 pm.
6 Cavendish Dr, Manukau, Ph: 275 5568.
241 Ti Rakau Dr, Pakuranga, Ph: 272 2655.

RAINBOWS END

The biggest playground for everybody's children, and the child in all of us is Rainbow's End, a park with adventure rides of all kinds. The kids would love to take the plunge on the popular log flume ride, scream along with dozens of others on the huge pirate galleon swing, or hold on tight on the country's only Double Corkscrew roller coaster. For quieter moments you and they could bump around in dodgem boats, or rev around a mini-race track in high-powered sounding karts (see '20 Top Attractions', p. 105).

MINI GOLF

A great way for the whole family to spend an hour or two. Loads of fun for both the golf pros amongst us, and those who might need a little help.

Lilliputt Mini Golf
3 Tamaki Dr, Auckland Waterfront, Ph: 524 4096.
Open: 7 days, summer 10 am–10 pm, winter Mon to Thur 10 am–5 pm
Fri to Sun 10 am–9 pm. Costs: adults $8, children $5, students $6.

Golf Today
Centre of Ellerslie Racecourse, Greenlane, East Remuera, Ph: 522 2124.
Open: 7 days, 8 am–8.30 pm, Sat/Sun 8 am–8 pm (winter hrs). Costs: adults $6, children (under 12) $4.

FAMILY RESTAURANTS

Sometimes it pays to know in advance whether your restaurant of choice is child-friendly! The following 'family restaurants' can be relied upon to offer food that will appeal to kids or even to supply separate children's menus. Many also have children's adventure playgrounds attached.

Pizza Hut
199 Lincoln Rd, Henderson, Ph: 837 4030.
50 Northcote Rd, Northcote, Ph: 480 0037.
490 Pakuranga Highway, Pakuranga, Ph: 535 6834.

McDonald's
Shore City Galleria, Takapuna, Ph: 489 6019.
Two Double Seven Broadway, Newmarket, Ph: 520 2929.
St Lukes Shopping Centre, Sandringham, Ph: 846 5160.
102 Gt North Rd, Grey Lynn, Ph: 361 0020.
Lynmall Foodcourt, New Lynn, Ph: 827 5594.

Cobb & Co
Poenamo Hotel, Northcote Rd, Northcote, Ph: 480 6109.
Elm St, Avondale, Ph: 828 1179.
Reeves Rd, Pakuranga, Ph: 576 9079.

Valentines Licensed Buffet Restaurants
290 Dominion Rd, Mt Eden, Ph: 630 6633.
111–115 Lincoln Rd, Henderson, Ph: 836 7000.
180 Wairau Rd, Glenfield, Ph: 444 5150.

Cultural Delights

In terms of the more uplifting experiences of mind and soul, Auckland – brash, commercial, latté-sipping – used to be thought of as a kind of 'Down Under-Los Angeles'. But those critics (who seem to have last been here in Victorian times) would today find the city abuzz with cultural activities, even if some inhabitants mightn't know of them.

MUSIC

Classical

For classical music buffs, the resident Auckland Philharmonia Orchestra presents world-ranking soloists and both the traditional classical and innovative repertoire throughout the year. There are usually more than 25 concerts a year, principally at the Auckland Town Hall and Aotea Centre.

The New Zealand Symphony Orchestra also performs at least 15 concerts a year in Auckland. Chamber music from leading international string quartets and other small ensembles can be heard throughout the year.

Visiting musical stars and other classical concerts are all publicised in the entertainment pages of the morning paper, the *New Zealand Herald* (particularly on Saturdays).

Rock

There are plenty of live music venues delivering all kinds of New Zealand rock, pop, acoustic and dance/DJ music. Some to sample:

The King's Arms Tavern, 59 France St, Newton, Ph: 373 3240.

Temple, 486 Queen St, Auckland Central, Ph: 377 4866.

Java Jive, Cnr Ponsonby Rd & Pompallier Tce, Ponsonby, Ph: 376 5870.

Galatos, 17 Galatos St, off Karangahape Rd, Newton, Ph: 303 1928.

The Dog's Bollix, 582 Karangahape Rd, Newton, Ph: 376 4600.

St James Complex, 312 Queen St, Auckland Central, Ph: 377 7666.

The Masonic Tavern, 29 King Edward Pde, Devonport, Ph: 445 0485.

Big rock shows are held at various venues around the city. Check the newspaper for event details.

Jazz/Blues

Jazz fans will find the hot local groups most often at pubs, bars and restaurants, in lieu of any regular Jazz club in Auckland (unsuccessfully tried). Some bars that regularly feature Jazz and Blues musicians are:

London Bar in the Civic Tavern, Cnr Wellesley and Queen Sts, Auckland Central, Ph: 373 3684.

The Jazz Bar, 350 Queen St, Auckland Central, Ph: 309 2512.

The New Brew Tavern, Cnr Rosedale Rd and William Pickering Dr, Albany, Ph: 414 5450.

Gables Tavern, Cnr Jervois Rd and Kelmarna Ave, Herne Bay, Ph: 376 4994.

You can enjoy weekend, lunchtime and afternoon Jazz at many venues including:

Iguacu Restaurant & Bar, 269 Parnell Rd, Parnell, Ph: 358 4804.

Horse and Trap bar/restaurant, 3 Enfield St, Mt Eden, Ph: 630 3055.

ART

The Auckland Art Gallery

Cnr Wellesley and Kitchener Sts, Auckland Central, Ph: 307 7700.

Open: 10 am–5 pm daily, free entry. New Gallery Free admission to ground floor galleries.

The Auckland Art Gallery lays claim to the largest and most comprehensive collection of New Zealand and international art in the country. The collections are divided between two buildings – the main collection in the French renaissance-style principal gallery, and across the road, the New Gallery hosts smaller shows of contemporary art. Free guided tours of the main gallery's collection exhibition every day at 2 pm. Special and touring exhibitions are frequent, with a small charge for entry.

Gallery Guide

AUCKLAND CENTRAL

GranthamGalleries

First floor, Premier Building, Cnr Queen St & Durham St East, Auckland Central, Ph: 308 9239.

Website: www.granthamgalleries.com

Open: Mon & Sat 11 am–3 pm, Tue to Fri 11 am–5 pm, or by appointment.

New contemporary fine art and mixed media from both well-established and emerging artists. Monthly exhibitions.

Artspace

Level 1, 300 Karangahape Rd, Auckland Central, Ph: 303 4965.

Website: www.artspace.org.nz

Open Tues to Fri 10 am–6 pm, Sat 11 am–4 pm (Feb to Nov).

Closed during exhibition changes. Contemporary New Zealand and international art.

Compendium Gallery

5 Lorne St, Auckland Central, Ph: 300 3212.
Website: www.compendium.co.nz
Open: Mon to Thurs 10 am–5.30 pm, Fri 10 am–7 pm, Sat 10 am–4 pm.
Contemporary New Zealand craft: glass, wood, jewellery, garments and sculpture. Wide range of art and corporate gift choices.

George Fraser Gallery

25a Princes St, Auckland Central, Ph: 367 7163.
Website: www.georgefraser.auckland.ac.nz
Open: Wed to Fri 11 am–4 pm, Sat 11 am–2 pm.
Showcases recent developments in contemporary art practice associated with Elam School of Fine Arts at the University of Auckland.

Gow Langsford Gallery

Cnr Kitchener St & Wellesley St East, Auckland Central, Ph: 303 4290.
Website: www.gowlangsfordgallery.co.nz
Open: Mon to Fri 10 am–6 pm, Sat 11 am–3 pm.
Exhibits both contemporary New Zealand paintings and sculpture, as well as international works by selected artists.

Oedipus Rex Gallery

1st Floor, 32 Lorne St, Auckland Central, Ph: 379 0588.
Website: www.orexgallery.co.nz
Open: Mon & Sat 11 am–3 pm, Tues to Fri 11 am–5 pm.
Contemporary New Zealand painting and sculpture.

Ferner Galleries City (formerly Portfolio Gallery)

10 Lorne St, Auckland Central, Ph: 379 0145.
Website: www.fernergalleries.co.nz
Open: Mon to Fri 9.30 am–5.30 pm, Sat 10 am–4 pm.
Quality New Zealand original artworks, with a focus on contemporary art, and works on paper.

The Lane Gallery

12 O'Connell St, Auckland Central, Ph: 302 5295.
Website: www.lanegallery.co.nz
Open: Mon to Fri 10 am–6 pm, Sat 10 am–4 pm.
Specialises in contemporary New Zealand artwork: paintings, hand-finished artists' prints, and sculpture. The emphasis is on imagery that is reflective of New Zealand, the Pacific, Maori culture and Asian influences.

INNER SUBURBS
PARNELL

Artis Gallery

280 Parnell Rd, Parnell, Ph: 303 1090.
Website: www.artisgallery.biz
Open: Mon to Fri 9 am–6 pm, Sat 10 am–4 pm, Sundays by appointment.
A contemporary gallery with a strong exhibition focus, Artis Gallery represents a diverse range of leading New Zealand painters, sculptors and photographers.

Ferner Galleries Parnell

367 Parnell Rd, Parnell, Ph: 309 0107.
Website: www.fernergalleries.co.nz
Open: Mon to Fri 9.30 am–5.30 pm, Sat 10 am–4 pm, Sun 12 pm–4 pm.
Quality New Zealand original artworks, from traditional to contemporary.

Jonathan Grant Galleries

280 Parnell Rd, Parnell, Ph: 308 9125.
Website: www.artis-jgg.co.nz
Open: Mon to Fri 9 am–6 pm, Sat 10 am–4 pm.
Specialises in 19th- and 20th-century English, Continental and antipodean paintings and historical New Zealand watercolours.

Warwick Henderson Gallery

32 Bath St, Parnell, Ph: 309 7513.
Website: www.warwickhenderson.co.nz
Open: Mon to Fri 10 am–5.30 pm, Sat & Sun 10 am–4 pm.
Specialises in fine contemporary and period New Zealand art, housed in an award-winning purpose-built gallery.

NEWMARKET

Morgan Street Gallery

9 Morgan St, Newmarket, Ph: 358 0577.
Website: www.morgan-street-gallery.co.nz
Open: Mon to Fri 9 am–5.30 pm, Sat 10 am–3.30 pm.
A contemporary art gallery, representing New Zealand and Pacific artists.

Studio of Contemporary Art

5–7 Kingdon St, Newmarket, Ph: 529 0533.
Website: www.soca.co.nz
Open: Mon to Fri 10 am–5 pm, Sat 10 am–3 pm.
Specialises in New Zealand paintings, prints and sculpture.

PONSONBY/GREY LYNN

Garry Nash Sunbeam Glassworks

70 Mackelvie St, Ponsonby, Ph: 376 2744.
Website: www.garrynash.co.nz
Open: Mon to Fri 9 am–4 pm, Sat 10 am–2 pm.
Studio of glass artist Garry Nash who has exhibited in the United States, Australia and Japan. (Works for sale.)

Masterworks Gallery

77 Ponsonby Rd, Ponsonby, Ph: 378 1256.
Website: www.masterworksgallery.com
Open: Mon to Fri 9.30 am–5.30 pm, Sat 10 am–5 pm, Sun 11 am–4 pm.
Specialises in contemporary New Zealand studio glass, ceramics and jewellery.

EASTERN SUBURBS

John Leech Gallery

360 Remuera Rd, Remuera, Ph: 523 1325.
Open: Mon to Wed & Fri 9 am–5 pm, Thurs 9 am–6 pm, Sat 9.30 am–12.30 pm.
Traditional-style paintings.

WESTERN SUBURBS

Packing Shed Gallery & Café

99 Parrs Cross Rd, Henderson, Ph: 835 1557.
Open: 7 days 10 am–4 pm.
Painting, pottery, sculpture, glasswork, jewellery, prints, woodware, bone carvings and New Zealand souvenirs mainly by West Auckland artists.

NORTH SHORE

Art By The Sea

Cnr King Edward Pde & Church St (opposite Masonic Tavern), Devonport, Ph: 445 6665.
Website: www.artbythesea.co.nz
Open: 7 days 10 am–5 pm.
A wide selection of paintings, prints and decorative arts by New Zealand artists, including jewellery, ceramics, glass, wood, sculptures, garden pots etc.

THEATRE

The Auckland Theatre Company stages about eight to 10 contemporary productions a year at various venues (it's a nomadic company) particularly at Maidment Theatre at the University, Ph: 308 2383, and The Herald Theatre at the Aotea Centre, Ph: 309 2677.

Watch for alternative local theatre at the Maidment Theatre studio, or Silo Theatre, Ph: 373 5151. Or stand-up New Zealand comedy at The Classic Comedy & Bar, Ph: 373 4321.

DANCE/ MUSICALS/ SHOWS

The Civic Theatre, Ph: 309 2677, the Aotea Centre, Ph: 309 2677 and the Sky City Theatre, Ph: 363 6000 are frequent venues for local and visiting performances, particularly the Royal New Zealand Ballet. Check the newspaper for coming events.

BOOKS

New Zealand books and magazines are available in abundance at some excellent bookshops around town. Auckland offers everything from the big-range corner stores of Whitcoulls (cnr Queen and Victoria Sts, Auckland Central) and Borders (291–297 Queen St, Auckland Central) to more specialised shops where local writing is a passion, such as Unity Books for the latest New Zealand literature (19 High St, Auckland Central, Ph: 307 0731), Parsons Bookshop for an art focus (cnr Wellesley and Lorne Sts, Ph: 303 1557), Jason Books for great second-hand New Zealand books (upstairs, 3 Lorne St, Auckland Central, Ph: 379 0266), and the Women's Bookshop for know-ledgeable help to find some of the best New Zealand writing around (proprietor Carole Beu has been twice named

New Zealand Bookseller of the Year; 105 Ponsonby Rd, Ponsonby, Ph: 376 4399).

For a change of pace, the Auckland Public Library occasionally displays some of its valuable book and manuscript collection (Milton, Shakespeare and early colonial New Zealand works among them).

MUSEUMS

Auckland Museum is the biggie, but for a change of perspective, sample these smaller museums:

Naval Museum
Spring St, Devonport, Ph: 445 5186.
Open: 7 days, free entry (optional donation).
Nostalgia and naval militaria relieved with many human interest stories.

The Museum of Transport, Technology and Social History (MOTAT)
Great North Rd, Western Springs, Ph: 846 0199.
Open: 7 days, 10 am–5 pm. Costs: adults $10, children (5–16 yrs) $5.
Volunteers gallantly maintain this preserve of old buses, planes, trains, trams, machinery, communications equipment, colonial shops and aviation memorabilia. Best bits for kids: getting into the cab of the 90-tonne K900 steam train, travelling on the tram, playing in the Science and Technology Centre.

Howick Historical Village
Bell's Rd, Lloyd Elsmore Park, Pakuranga, Ph: 576 9506.
Costs: adults $10, children $5.
Website: www.fencible.org.nz
In this recreated village of settlers' 'fencible' cottages, there are vivid scenes of life in colonial New Zealand and even more lively stories.

New Zealand National Maritime Museum
Quay St, Auckland, Ph: 373 0800.

Check out New Zealand's Maori, Polynesian and European maritime history, from the first journeys of the Maori to our shores, to the English immigrants at the turn of the 19th century. Actors tell you the story, there's maritime art, the history of the America's Cup, and the chance to ride in one of the museum's boats, moored outside.

OUTDOOR AND CIVIC SCULPTURE

Auckland has accumulated a surprising amount of contemporary sculpture, provided you know where to look. Corporate sponsorship has supported the creation of some of the larger works visible in the foyers of various buildings. Of note is the art in the Royal and Sun Alliance foyer (48 Shortland St, Auckland Central) with its wall of New Zealand quotations. Also check out:

Seven tekoteko (freestanding statue figures), America's Cup Village, Viaduct Basin, Quay St, Auckland Central.

Stainless-steel Double L Gyratory (1984) by George Rickey. Outside courtyard, Auckland Art Gallery, Kitchener St, Auckland Central.

Throwback (1988) by Neil Dawson. Albert Park, Kitchener St, Auckland Central.

Gateway by Selwyn Muru, Aotea Square, Queen St, Auckland Central.

Fountain by Terry Stringer, Aotea Square, Queen St, Auckland Central.

Aotea Tapestry by Robert Ellis, Aotea Centre, ground floor.

Circus of Life mural by Jenny Dolezel, Aotea Centre, circle foyer.

Sky City casino has a surprising number of modern artworks, including: Mahi Whakairo (decorated canoe hull) by Lyonel Grant, ground floor foyer wall. Atrium Waterfall by Gordon Moller, ground floor foyer. Te-Ika-a-Maui (The Fish of Maui) by Dick Frizzell, foyer wall by ground floor escalator.

Fountain by Greer Twiss, bronze (1969), Symonds St park, cnr Symonds St and Karangahape Rd, Auckland Central.

Festival Time

Auckland is a city of diversity, and there is something going on – somewhere – most of the time. Whether it's scintillating sailing, fabulous food or wonderful wines, you'll find the city and the suburbs abuzz with entertainment.

Pasifika Festival, 13 March 2004.
Western Springs Park, Great North Rd, Western Springs, Ph: 353 9518.
Website: www.akcity.govt.nz/pasifika
Wonderful lakeside setting resounds with the music of Polynesia, as Pacific Island groups perform throughout the day on several stages. Stalls sell ethnic food, music, clothing. Free entry.

Pasifika Festival

Chinese Lantern Festival.

Ellerslie Flower Show.

Parnell Rose Gardens Festival, every November.

Parnell Rose Gardens, Dove-Myer Robinson Park, Gladstone Rd, Parnell.

Strolling musicians, dancers on stage and other performers enliven the first blush of more than 350 varieties of rose beginning to bloom. Free entry to the gardens and the Auckland Rose Society's exhibition and competition in St Mary's Church. A free loop bus links the various venues.

Ellerslie Flower Show, every November.

Auckland Regional Botanic Gardens, 100 Hill Rd, Manurewa (follow signs from Manukau City motorway exit, only public site entrance off Everglade Dr), Ph: 309 7875.

Website: www.ellerslieflowershow.co.nz

Claimed to be the largest gardening and live event show in the Southern Hemisphere, the Ellerslie Flower Show attracts 60,000 local and overseas visitors every year. More than 300 exhibitors, and marquees displaying floral art (Christmas theme), garden makeover ideas, outdoor garden designs, exotic plant exhibits and future horticulture. Beginning with a trade preview and media day, and culminating with the grand plant sale. Ticket prices range from $26 for a half day to $33 for a full day. Concessions are available.

Auckland Highland Games, every November.

Three Kings Reserve, Three Kings.

Ph: 379 1352 (Auckland City events line)

Auckland City has hosted these games for the past 20 years and in recent times up to 10,000 people have gone along to watch the dancing, pipe bands, hammer-throwing, caber-tossing and haggis-hurling.

Santa Parade, every November/December.

Queen St, Auckland Central.

Expect to be one of hundreds of thousands as the children watch cartoon characters, clowns, and Santa himself in this annual parade which has a legacy of 50-plus years behind

it. Arrive early for a ground-level spot with a good view (for smallest family members).

Sky City Starlight Symphony, 7.30–10.30 pm, 14 Feb 2004.
Auckland Domain.

A free outdoor concert featuring a range of top local and international operatic and contemporary performers. Around 200,000 people go along for the fun, so make sure you arrive early enough to get a good position.

Coca-Cola Christmas in the Park, every (mid) December.
Auckland Domain.

The annual Coca-Cola Christmas in the Park features New Zealand's favourite entertainers. It's a free night of music, dancing and fireworks to get you in the festive mood.

The New Zealand Herald Anniversary Day Regatta, Auckland Anniversary Day (last Monday of every January).
Waitemata Harbour, races from 10.30 am to dusk. Check the *New Zealand Herald* for details during January.

The City of Sails writ large. The Auckland Anniversary Regatta began on 18 September 1840, when a sale of land by Apihai te Kawau and his tribe to European settlers was celebrated with three races: two for European boats, one for canoes. Unofficial regattas were held each year until 1850 when the Auckland Anniversary Regatta was inaugurated to celebrate the founding of Auckland. Yachts of every class have turned out en masse to race on Anniversary Day and, Anniversary holiday regattas of 1000 boats were not uncommon at its peak. Great viewing from any vantage-point around the harbour.

Lantern Festival, 6–8 February 2004.
Albert Park, Auckland Central, Ph: 470 8704.

In an innovative move, the Auckland City Council supports a lantern festival based on the model of similar events in

Asia. Competitions and displays of lanterns from Asia and local sources. Another sign of the city's increasing diversity. Food, fortune-telling, martial arts displays and free entry.

Devonport Food and Wine Festival, 21 & 22 February 2004.
Windsor Reserve, Devonport, Ph: 445 0685.
Website: www.devonportwinefestival.co.nz

The road is closed to join two halves of Windsor Reserve into a major food and wine pleasure garden. Wine shops and individual winemakers will provide tastings during this festival and a huge variety of food is available from caterers and food companies. Open Sat and Sun 11 am–6 pm. Free entry, but you'll need to buy an official glass to be able to drink the wines (licensing age limit of 18 applies).

Teddy Bears' Picnic, every February.
Auckland Domain, Park Rd, Auckland Central.

For 20 years this free gathering has taken place of the city's toy bears and their owners and friends. Some 60,000 to 80,000 bear-owners and families vie for prizes for best-dressed and most-loved bears. Strolling players entertain and bouncing castles, face-painters and rides operate beside three stages providing non-stop children's fun.

Music in Parks, Jan to Mar 2004.
Various locations.

A series of free concerts held in a variety of city and suburban parks. There's a concert for every taste, including jazz, classical, blues, soul, rock and Latin music, and local industry icons are often involved. Check the *New Zealand Herald* for details.

Dancing in the Street, One Friday evening in each of Jan, Feb, Mar 2004.

Free street concerts in the central city, held in association with Music in Parks. Check the *New Zealand Herald* for details.

Auckland International Cultural Festival, 10 am–5 pm, 29 Feb 2004.
Potters Park, Mt Eden.

Travel the world without leaving the city. This free festival showcases the diversity of Auckland's residents. Music, song, dance, arts and crafts from over 30 nations are on display throughout the day, and a wonderful array of traditional food can be obtained, including Asian, African, Indian and European.

Waiheke Island Wine Festival, 31 Jan to 1 Feb, 2004.
Book at Ticketek (Ph: 307 5000) or Fullers offices.
Website: www.waihekewine.co.nz/festival/

Waiheke Island's temperate maritime climate has been discovered by winemakers and now more than 20 vineyards flourish in this special area. The hilly settings might be tough for harvesting, but provide some marvellous vistas across the vines and the surrounding harbour. Top restaurants in several vineyards.

Waiheke Island Jazz Festival, every Easter weekend.
Ph: 0800 529 933.
Website: www.waihekejazz.co.nz

For three and a half days, venues across this Hauraki Gulf island resound with every kind of Jazz from traditional and Dixie through to mainstream modern. Music and food feast that has thousands flocking here.

Auckland Film Festival, every July.
Website: www.auckland.nzff.co.nz

The Auckland International Film Festival was set up more than 30 years ago, and now draws a total of more than 80,000 viewers during the 16-day, 140-plus film feast.

Expect everything from the first screenings of New Zealand films, classics (usually including a silent film with live orchestral accompaniment), to documentaries that never make it to TV or mainstream cinema.

Shop Till You Drop

Not so long ago, shopping in Auckland meant 'going to town' (typically Queen St and the inner city), between Monday and Friday only, and being 'dealt to' rather than served. Dedicated shoppers went to Sydney on shopping weekends, or threw in the towel and emigrated.

Now, Auckland's best shops are as good as you will find anywhere, nearly all are open seven days a week with 'late-night shopping' on either Thursday or Friday until 9 pm, and there are early warning signs of a service tradition developing.

MECCAS

Albany Megacentre Mega Mecca
Don McKinnon Drive, Albany (end of Northern Motorway).
A bombastic, United States-scale (you'll need to drive between stores) shopping city on Auckland's frontier, Albany. Rebel Sports, The Warehouse, Farmers Home Centre, Pumpkin Patch and many, many more – big names with big stores and an emphasis on the cheaper end of the market. It's shopping as safari and not the place for service-with-a-smile sentimentalists.

High St/Vulcan Lane Fashion Mecca, Auckland Central.
Auckland's best-known fashion designers huddle together for warmth within a few square metres of the CBD. From the oh-so-upmarket styles of Zambesi and Workshop, to the buttoned-down business wear of Working Style, to the classical quality of Keith Matheson, to the retro garments at Smoove and Harlem 23. Also worth a look: Ricochet, Stella

Gregg, Kate Sylvester, Glory, and Cody. Branches of some shops have now migrated to Ponsonby Road and Parnell.

Karangahape Rd Funky Mecca, Auckland Central.

K' Rd has always threatened to become respectable but never quite got around to it. From the sex shops and nightclubs at one end to the idiosyncratic curio shops, alternative music and clothing outlets, Pacific Island fish and produce stores, Indian fabric retailers, and design stores at the other, K'Rd is the place to shop if you are looking for something different from the mainstream fare.

Newmarket Classy Mecca, Broadway, Newmarket.

Newmarket is the retail centre of choice for Auckland's smart set. The emphasis is on fashion but you'll also find books, music, toys, sportswear, cosmetics, quality food and some quirky one-offs. The many fine cafés provide some relief from the retail frenzy.

Onehunga Bargain Mecca, Dressmart, Onehunga.

The always-teetering-on-the-brink-of-trendiness suburb of Onehunga boasts a collection of factory shops featuring some of the biggest clothing names in town. You can pick up bargains by the likes of Keith Matheson and Pumpkin Patch.

SHOPPING MALL CITY

The safety and comfort in enclosed shopping malls may be part of their attraction – it's also cool in summer, warm in winter. The Westfield Shopping Town brand is the biggest locally.

Westfield Shopping Town, St Lukes, St Lukes Rd, Mt Albert.

Lynmall Shopping Centre, Great North Rd, New Lynn.

Westfield Shopping Town, Glenfield Mall, Cnr Glenfield Rd & Downing St, Glenfield, North Shore City.

277, Broadway, Newmarket.

Botany Town Centre, Botany Downs, East Tamaki.

Westfield Shopping Town, Manukau City Shopping Centre, Cnr Great South and Wiri Station Rds, Manukau City, South Auckland.

DEPARTMENT STORES

Smith & Caughey's
253–261 Queen St, Auckland Central, Ph: 377 4770.
225 Broadway, Newmarket, Ph: 524 8049.

Last grand old department store in central city. Mix of the upmarket and trendy, and the conservative. Older shop staff call customers 'Sir' and 'Madam' and Caughey family members still patrol the shop. Twice-yearly 'fairs' offer classy bargains in January and July.

DFS Duty Free Galleria
Customhouse Building, Cnr Customs and Albert Sts, Auckland Central, Ph: 0800 388 937.

Set in one of Auckland's best-preserved historic buildings, the Galleria offers duty-free shoppers one of the city's best ranges of cosmetics and perfumes, plus upmarket fashions and accessories in a spacious, gracious old building.

The Warehouse
Downtown Shopping Centre, Lower Albert St, Auckland Central, Ph: 309 6996; 22 other branches (check phone book).

The five-and-dime store for the new millennium. It is all cheap and a lot of it is good quality, partly thanks to the practice of parallel importing which lets the store bring in fancy imports at a fraction of the price their authorised distributors have to charge. The perfect place to gift buy for those 10 nephews and nieces back home. Don't dress up.

MEN'S FASHION

Zambesi
Cnr Vulcan Lane & O'Connell St, Auckland Central, Ph: 303 1701.
2 Teed St, Newmarket, Ph: 523 1000.

Helmut Lang, Paul Smith, Comme des Garcons, plus top quality wear from some of New Zealand's best designers. The shop packs a surprising variety of clothing into a space the size of a large wardrobe and the staff have a knack for 'finding items that suit you, Sir'. They will even have you feeling virtuous for spending that much money.

Saks
254 Broadway, Newmarket, Ph: 520 7634.
Escada, Versace, Hugo Boss and Ermenegildo Zegna – Saks specialises in imported fashions from leading international designers. It's a one-stop quality shop for any-occasion wear and sets an Auckland service benchmark. They will even open outside normal hours by appointment.

WOMEN'S FASHION

World
57 High St, Auckland Central, Ph: 373 3034.
World (Men) 47 High St, Auckland Central, Ph: 377 8331.
175 Ponsonby Rd, Ponsonby, Ph: 360 4544.
20 Remuera Rd, Remuera, Ph: 524 0424
Smart and silly, witty and serious, World's designs are everything fashion should be. From very proper jackets that would be at home in any office to over-the-top high-camp party frocks, and carefully selected accessories, everything here embodies the ethos that clothes and life are to be enjoyed, not aspired to.

Karen Walker
15 O'Connell St, Auckland Central, Ph: 309 6299.
6 Balm St, Newmarket, Ph: 522 4286.
Austere in atmosphere, global in outlook, New Zealand in sensitivity – and that's just the design of the shop. Walker's fashions insist on being judged only by the highest international standards, thank you very much. Everyone

should have at least one of her superlative garments in their wardrobe.

Scotties

3 Lorne St, Auckland Central, Ph: 366 1664.

2 Blake St, Ponsonby, Ph: 379 6617.

Marilyn Sainty is famous for her always flattering designs in sumptuous fabrics and tasteful colours. It's a sophisticated, subtly simple, international look that somehow seems to suit everyone who wears it. The shops also carry a selected range of imported, big-name international labels.

Trelise Cooper

201 Quay St, Waterfront, Ph: 366 1964.

536 Parnell Rd, Parnell, Ph: 366 1962.

100 Richmond Rd, Ponsonby, Ph: 360 9578.

Designer Trelise Cooper is a mass of wild blonde curls and a quiet riot of colour, a bit like her clothes which are created to reflect the many moods of women. Her holistic approach has served her three labels well: the Trelise Cooper label for high fashion; Luscious, 'a collection for the more voluptuous figure because not only size-10 women want to be gorgeous'; and Cooper, driven by the young designers.

KIDS

Pumpkin Patch

377 Manukau Rd, Epsom, Ph: 623 1303.

9 other branches (Ph: 274 7088 for head office).

This New Zealand children's label has made a success of a notoriously difficult industry. The clothes are not dirt cheap but their quality and durability make them better value than many cheaper equivalents. Styles are smart without being precocious and shops always seem to have just what you're looking for.

SHOES

Minnie Cooper
78 Ponsonby Rd, Ponsonby, Ph: 376 3058.

Designed and made in New Zealand of quality components sourced from around the world, Minnie Cooper's shoes find favour with everyone. The ranges are small but comprehensive, tending to classic with a subtle twist, well-sized for real feet, and there is also a good selection of bags and clothing.

JEWELLERY

Fingers Contemporary Jewellery
2 Kitchener St, Auckland Central, Ph: 373 3974.

Fingers showcases the work of more than 40 established and emerging jewellers in styles ranging from the outrageous to the conservative. You'll find work in bone, jade, mother of pearl and paua, all distinctly New Zealand.

GIFTS & SOUVENIRS

Out of New Zealand
45 Queen St, Auckland Central, Ph: 358 2337.

Calling them souvenirs doesn't do justice to the beautifully crafted items sold in this unique store. Look for exquisite writing compendia in native rimu timber, and extraordinarily detailed model sailing ships. Definitely in a class of its own.

The Great New Zealand Shop
7 Queen St, Auckland Central, Ph: 377 3009.
Crowne Plaza Hotel, 128 Albert St, Auckland Central, Ph: 377 6966.
Victoria Park Market, Ph: 379 4549.
Auckland International Airport, Ph: 256 6650.

It's all here – cuddly kiwifruit, kiwi pendants made of paua shell, plastic Maori maiden dolls, jade pussycats, scenic coasters, sheepskin-lined slippers, T-shirts, T-shirts and T-shirts. From tacky trinkets to upmarket mementos, these are what most of us mean when we say 'souvenir'.

CRAFTS

Pauanesia
35 High St, Auckland Central, Ph: 366 7282.

There's more than meets the eye in this shoebox of a shop. All products have a strong Maori/Pasifika flavour and include the likes of handwoven kits, mirrors framed in fantastic paua shell creations, and tapa-patterned ceramics and cushions handpainted with shell designs. You will pay well for the quality and rarity of some of these items.

ANTIQUES

Visit Manukau Rd, Epsom, for a wide range of antique shops, and also check out www.portobello.com.au/info/nz-auckland for the complete list of antique shops in Auckland.

BOOKS

Borders Books & Music
291–297 Queen St, Auckland, Ph: 309 3377.
Open: Sun to Thurs 10 am–10 pm, Fri to Sat 10 am–12 pm.

Great selection of books, records and magazines.

Dymocks
Atrium on Elliott, 21 Elliott St, Auckland Central, Ph: 379 9919, also at Newmarket and Glenfield.

A bookshop where books are the priority, not just part of a product mix.

Hard to Find (But Worth The Effort) Bookstore
Central City, 238 Karangahape Rd, Ph: 303 0555.
81A Victoria Rd, Devonport, Ph: 446 0300.
171 The Mall, Onehunga, Ph: 634 4340.

This is everything a second-hand bookshop is supposed to be – groaning shelves, slightly musty, labyrinthine layout, classics at bargain prices plus rare and collectable treasures. It boasts the largest stock of any second-hand bookshop, so allow plenty of browsing time.

Unity Books
19 High St, Auckland Central, Ph: 307 0731.

Verging on shrine status among the local literati, this is where Auckland's writers come to buy – and often launch – their books. It has the latest succès d'estime from overseas along with what is probably Auckland's best selection of local fiction, non-fiction and poetry. Helpful, well-informed staff.

MUSIC

Marbecks Record Shop
15 Queen's Arcade, Auckland Central, Ph: 379 0444.

Two stores sit a few doors apart: one is for classical, the other for everything else. The stock is the city's most comprehensive and the staff (gasp!) know what you're talking about. There is also a fine range of operas on video.

Real Groovy Records
438 Queen St, Auckland Central, Ph: 302 3940.

The poky used-LP shop has mutated into the ideal hyperstore for the under-25s (there are books, clothes and magazines as well). The stock covers essential new, rare second-hand and the occasional gem that's fallen off the back of a mixing desk. The only place to go for that hard-to-find or deleted CD to fill the gap in your collection.

GOURMET FOODS

Sabato
55 Normanby Rd, Mt Eden, Ph: 630 8151.

Excellent imported food selection.

Zarbo Delicatessen and Café
24 Morrow St, Newmarket, Ph: 520 2721.

Food, good coffee, and quality ingredients. Its own range includes pasta sauces, wonderful dressings, chutneys and conserves.

WINE

Good wine is freely available in supermarkets in New Zealand and smaller wine boutiques in the suburbs, but for specialist advice, try one of the following.

Glengarry Wines
Victoria Park, 118 Wellesley St, Auckland Central, Ph: 308 8346.
139 Ponsonby Rd, Ponsonby, Ph: 378 8252.
Cnr Mayoral Dr & Wellesly St, Auckland Central, Ph: 379 8416.
Specialist wine shops which carry a large range of local wines as well as imports. The company set up the Glengarry Wine Academy to train staff, and now offers general public courses for beginners as well. Frequent wine tastings are held at the shops.

Fine Wine Delivery Company
201 Hobson St, Auckland Central, Ph: 377 2300 or 0800 FINEWINE (0800 346 394).
Website: www.finewineonline.co.nz
An online specialist, as the name suggests, but you can still call in at their Hobson Street warehouse and buy by the bottle in person. The knowledgeable Fine Wine team taste about 130 wines a month to make sure they can recommend them to customers. Check out when they hold their regular and popular wine tastings and wine events.

La Barrique
154 Remuera Rd, Remuera, Ph: 524 6666.
Unique on the New Zealand wine scene, La Barrique has around 3000 wines and Auckland's largest temperature-controlled cellar. Locals can enjoy a variety of special services, and visitors won't find a better place to be initiated into the glories of New Zealand's internationally lauded drops. Staff are conspicuously well-informed and non-threatening.

Market Time

Markets often mean a bargain of some kind, but their character can also reflect an aspect of the city and the times. Auckland has a smattering of good markets where you can expect everything from flash to trash. Markets also tend to come and go, so check out the Auckland Travel and Information Centre for pamphlets and information about any new markets that might be on the scene when you're looking for one. Here's a sampling of some of Auckland's more appealing and more enduring markets (free entry unless otherwise stated):

Aotea Square Market

Aotea Square, Auckland Central, Ph: 307 5075.
Open: Fri & Sat 10 am–6 pm.
This all-weather, 2-day market is a council-approved attempt to brighten up the paved desert of Aotea Square (Terry Stringer's mountain-like fountain is the brave exception to Brutalist architectural surroundings). A colourful mix of casual and professional stallholders, selling everything from food and clothes to local and exotic crafts and jewellery (NZ bone carvings, paua, Pacific tapa, African work), and even pot-luck bargains (second-hand kitchenware from 50 cents to $5).

Avondale Market

Avondale Racecourse, Ash St, Avondale. Infoline Ph: 818 4931.
Open: Sun 6 am–noon.
Takes place in rain, hail or sunshine. Very popular. Wide

range of goods and food. If you want to sell, $20 buys you a car space, $5 hires a trestle table. Sales of fish, shellfish, prepared food or animals not allowed. Top shopping site.

Collectors Market

Auckland Showgrounds, 217 Greenlane Rd West, Greenlane, Ph: 524 2462.
Website: www.collectorsmarketnz.com
Open: second Sunday of every month, 9 am–3 pm.

More than 100 stalls offering antiques and collectables, from big-ticket furniture items to $20 bargains, including china, toys, militaria, books and kitchen goods (castironware, green and cream enamelware). Sellers include collectors, merchants and independents trading on behalf of estates and owners. Out-of-town buyers from Wellington and Christchurch attend regularly. Parking $2, entry $5.

Karangahape Rd Street Market

Motorway overbridge, Karangahape Rd, Auckland Central.
Open: Sat 10 am–4pm.

Small, mostly clothes (new and secondhand), knick-knacks, some tapa cloths and Pacific Island baskets.

Mangere Market

Carpark, Mangere town centre, 93 Bader Dr (behind Farmers), Mangere, Ph: 275 7078.
Open: Sat 6 am–2 pm.

Polynesian character provides the relaxed atmosphere here where around 300 stalls produce the usual mix of food, vegetables, clothes and craft. You may strike it lucky with the occasional performance from a Pacific Island church choir, or cultural group at around 11.30 am.

St Heliers Bay Village Handcraft Market

Cnr Polygon & Turua Sts, St Heliers, Ph: 521 5671.
Open: 1st & 3rd Sunday of the month, 10am–4pm.
This 100 percent New Zealand-made, new craft goods market has been in existence for 14 years. More than 30 stalls sell – generally at wholesale prices – woodturning work, pottery, picture frames, knitwear, silver and paua jewellery and handmade soaps.

Otara Market

Carpark, Newbury St, off East Tamaki Rd, Otara, Ph: 274 0830.
Open: Sat 6am–noon.
Still the most characterful and most Polynesian of all the markets, although clothes bearing names like Tommy Hilfiger sit beside floral pattern fabrics, white churchgoing hats, fresh watercress and T-shirts of 'Samoa' and 'Taro power'. Early arrivals score just-picked native vegetable delicacy puha (sow thistle) delivered fresh from north of Auckland.

Takapuna Market

Central car park, Anzac St, Takapuna, Ph: 376 2367.
Open: Sun 6 am–noon.
Popularity sees stalls overflow into surrounding streets. Abundance of bargain flowers (be in early), organic fruit, vegetables, honey and bread from stallholders who travel from up north, ornaments, books and videos and, surprisingly, New Zealand-made clothes.

Victoria Park Market

210 Victoria St West, Auckland Central, Ph: 309 6911.
Website: www.victoria-park-market.co.nz
Open: 7 days 9 am–6 pm.
Solidly commercial, and more upmarket. Former city rubbish incinerator (built 1901) which also had stables (for horses which pulled the garbage carts) and its own electricity-

generating steam-boilers, heated by the rubbish-burning furnace. The rubbish burner was closed in 1972, and restored to become a market. Check out famous people's handprints in the concrete walkway. Top shopping site (see 'Shop Till You Drop', p. 139).

Waiheke Island Market

Ostend War Memorial Hall, cnr Ostend & Belgium Sts, Ostend, Ph: 372 5502.
Open: Sat 8 am–1.30 pm.

Aucklanders travel here for the homemade stoneground-flour bread. The market's true Waiheke Island flavour derives from alternative and community lifestyle – new and used clothing, local craft such as wooden toys, candles and candelabra, tarot and iridology readings, community fundraising stalls, native plant seedlings, vegetables. Steiner kindergarten runs the kitchen.

Sport + Exercise

Sport

SPECTATOR SPORTS – SUMMER

CRICKET

Auckland Cricket Association, Infoline Ph: 815 4869.
Website: www.aucklandcricket.co.nz

Eden Park is the main ground for international cricket games during the summer. Watch for the tour by Pakistan who are in New Zealand from 8 December–17 January 2004. They play a one-day international in Auckland on 3 January. South Africa are in New Zealand from 12 February–30 March 2004. They play two one-day internationals in Auckland (on 14 February and 28 February) and a test match from 18–22 March.

In the domestic competition, one-day and three-day games are held at Eden Park and North Harbour Stadium. The domestic season runs from November through to March with the one-day competition being held in January.

Catch club cricket at Victoria Park in the city as well as small grounds all around Auckland.

TENNIS

Auckland Tennis Association, Ph: 373 3623.
Website: www.aucklandtennis.co.nz

ASB Women's Classic 5–10 January 2004.
Website: www.asgclassic.co.nz

ASB Bank Tennis Centre, The Strand, Parnell.

This is the stand-out tournament in New Zealand for women's tennis. Big international drawcards like Anna Kournikova, as well as a host of rising stars, make this a must-see for anyone who loves the game.

Heineken Men's Open 12–17 January 2004.
ASB Bank Tennis Centre, The Strand, Parnell.

Website: www.heinekenopen.co.nz

Again, this is the premier men's tournament in New Zealand. Even bigger names appear here than in the women's tournament: Rudzetski, Kuerten, Safin, Ivanesivic, all vying for prize money of more than $NZ300,000. This tournament runs just before the Australian Open and is seen as an ideal warm-up by the international players.

SOFTBALL

Auckland Softball Association, Norana Ave, Mangere, Ph: 275 1552.
Website: www.softballauckland.org.nz

New Zealand's three-time world champion men's softball team the Black Sox are made up of players found batting, pitching and catching at softball diamonds all over the country, like Norana Ballpark in Mangere and Rosedale Park on the North Shore. Club games are played in summer with tournaments at Rosedale Park in January and March.

BASKETBALL

The New Zealand Breakers.
Website: www.nzbreakers.co.nz

Building on the international success of the Tall Blacks, basketball is riding a wave of popularity in New Zealand. Now,

the Harvey Norman New Zealand Breakers go up against Australia's best in the Australian National Basketball League. Home games are held at the North Shore Events Centre and the league runs from October 2003 through to mid February 2004. Great games, great action, great excitement – and a large dose of trans-Tasman rivalry to boot.

NETBALL

Websites: www.aucklandnetball.co.nz and www.netballnorthharbour.co.nz

One of the biggest sports in New Zealand by levels of participation, the national league highlights the peak of our netballing talent. Auckland has teams competing from both North Harbour and Auckland city.

GOLF

Holden New Zealand Open, 15–18 January 2003.
Auckland Golf Club, Otahuhu, Ph: 276 6149.

New Zealand's big tournament featuring some of the country's best as well as top players from the Australasian PGA tour. Usually includes some major name drawcards from the international tour; in 2002 Tiger Woods was the star. In 2004 the venue is the Grange Golf Club, in Papatoetoe.

SAILING

The major local regatta of the summer is The Auckland Anniversary Day Regatta on January 26. On that day more than 1000 yachts take to the water in a huge number of different classes from the smallest dinghies to big keelers.

But all year round, you can watch races taking place at different spots around the harbour for different classes.

SPECTATOR SPORTS – WINTER

RUGBY

Auckland Rugby Football Union, Ph: 815 4850.
Website: www.aucklandrugby.co.nz

North Harbour Rugby, Ph: 414 0230.
Website: www.harbourrugby.co.nz

Rugby is the winter religion for many New Zealanders, and those in Auckland who drink lattés at Ponsonby cafés are no exception in their enthusiasm.

Mid-year, every year, the Tri-Nations series between the All Blacks, their trans-Tasman cousins the Wallabies, and South Africa should see at least one game at Eden Park.

In the meantime, you can check out the Super 12 rugby action with the Auckland Blues (2003 champions) at Eden Park and North Harbour Stadium. Competition begins February.

The national provincial championship (NPC) games are held later in the year from August to the end of October.

Club games take place at rugby grounds all around the city during winter.

RUGBY LEAGUE

New Zealand Warriors, Ph: 526 8822.
Website: www.warriors.co.nz

The success of the New Zealand Warriors team in the Australian National Rugby League competition – they reached the Grand Final in 2002 – has allowed the side to gradually build up a following from just the dedicated fans to a much wider public audience. Catch home games at Ericsson Stadium during the winter season.

Auckland Rugby League, Ph: 379 5645.

Website: www.aucklandleague.co.nz

A very competitive and intense local competition runs nationwide over winter with several Auckland teams turning out to battle for the Bartercard Cup.

SOCCER

The Football Kingz, Ph: 845 6441.

Website: www.footballkingz.co.nz

In a similar set-up to the Warriors rugby league team, New Zealand has a soccer team playing in the Australian National League – the Football Kingz. The team is fully professional and contains players from New Zealand and Australia as well as some South American imports. Ericsson Stadium is home ground for the Kingz.

A 10-team national league runs over summer and a nationwide knockout tournament, the prestigious Chatham Cup, first contested for in 1923, is fiercely fought over by many Auckland and other New Zealand teams.

ALL YEAR ROUND

HORSE RACING

Race meetings take place once or twice every month at the two gallops courses (Ellerslie and Avondale) or the harness racing course (Alexandra Park, Greenlane).

Auckland Racing Club

Ellerslie Racecourse, 80–100 Ascot Ave, Greenlane, Ph: 524 4069.

Website: www.ellerslie.co.nz

Major gallops meetings each year are Ellerslie's New Zealand Mercedes Derby Day (Boxing Day) and Lion Red Auckland Cup Day (New Year's Day) and the Mercedes Great Northern Steeplechase Winter Carnival (Queen's Birthday weekend, June 7).

Avondale Jockey Club

Avondale Racecourse, 90 Ash St, Avondale. Ph: 828 3309.

Avondale's big month is December with the Avondale Gold Cup, Concorde Handicap and Avondale Guineas.

Auckland Trotting Club

Alexandra Park Raceway, Greenlane Rd, Epsom, Ph: 630 5660.

Website: www.alexpark.co.nz

Big feature races at Alexandra Park in December each year include the Great Northern Derby, Great Northern Oaks and Auckland Trotting Cup (31 December), and the Rowe Cup Carnival.

EQUESTRIAN

Auckland Airport Regency Three Day Event, every December.

Puhinui Reserve, near Auckland Airport, Manukau, Ph: 256 8969.

Website: www.3dayevent.co.nz

This is the premier equestrian eventing show in New Zealand. Big name local and international riders compete in cross-country, dressage and show-jumping. This year's event includes a variety of family entertainment, such as a climbing wall, claybird shooting, gumboot throwing, a fashion parade and a jousting display.

SPEEDWAY

Western Springs Speedway, Stadium Rd, Western Springs, Ph: 573 5543.

Website: www.springsspeedway.com

High-revving, skidding races on big dirt track includes motorbikes, midget cars, TQs (three-quarter midget cars) and sprint cars. Western Springs is the oldest motor racing venue in New Zealand (since 1929) with an international reputation that regularly draws teams of racers from Australia and the United States. The 30- and 50-lap derbies and three-country contests guarantee thrilling watching. International racing runs through January and February.

HAVE A GO YOURSELF

ROUND THE BAYS FUN RUN

Auckland Waterfront, 14 March 2004, Ph: 027 275 4904.
Website: www.roundthebays.co.nz (website operates Oct–Mar)

If you're in town in March and fancy a bit of exercise, have a look at, or take part in, the world-famous 'Round the Bays' run. Every year tens of thousands of Aucklanders take part in this run. It caters for all abilities and many people walk the Bays as they can finish the distance in two hours and still get their certificate. The 'run' is a distance of 8.5 km around Auckland's waterfront.

GYMS AND COMMUNITY RECREATION CENTRES

If you just have to work out, or need to burn off some of those holiday calories, check out the public gyms and recreation centres listed below. All offer a variety of equipment, programmes and classes. Many also have crèches and cafeterias attached.

Note: Recreation centres will often close on statutory or public holidays such as Christmas Day or New Year's Day. Check by phone that a centre is open before heading there.

Avondale College Facilities, 203 Rosebank Rd, Avondale, Ph: 828 9885.

ASB Stadium, cnr Kohimarama and Kepa Rds, Kohimarama, Ph: 521 0009.

East Coast Bays Leisure Centre, Bute Rd, Browns Bay, Ph: 478 3379.

North Shore Events Centre, Silverfield Rd (off Porana Rd), Glenfield, Ph: 443 8199.

YMCA Ellerslie Recreation Centre, Michaels Ave, Ellerslie, Ph: 579 4716.

YMCA Mt Albert Recreation Centre, 773 New North Rd, Mt Albert, Ph: 846 0788.

Youthtown, 68 Nelson St, Auckland Central, Ph: 379 5430.

Ru

Horse Raci

Round the Bays.

GOLF

New Zealand is a country extremely well suited to playing golf – with its rolling green hills and mild climate. There are many great courses to choose from, particularly in Auckland. Here's a selection:

Aviation Country Club

Tom Pearce Dr, Auckland Airport, Ph: 275 6265.

Open: 7 days, 7 am–5 pm.

Fees: $25 affiliated, $45 non-affiliated. Bookings essential, Ph: 275 4601. Hire: clubs, $15 (9 holes), $25 (18 holes).

Relatively flat course with some tight and challenging fairways. A good testing golf course but still manageable for the average player. Situated only minutes away from the international airport – watch jumbo jets drift by while you wait at the tee.

Chamberlain Park Public Golf Course

46A Linwood Ave, Mt Albert, Ph: 815 4999.

Open: 7 days. No bookings taken.

Fees: $22 Mon to Fri, $24 Sat, Sun & public holidays. Hire: clubs with trundlers $35 (full set), $15 (half set).

Auckland's most popular and accessible public course. Moderately easy, 1 or 2 steep holes and long par-5 fairways. Not many bunkers, the odd creek hazard. Expect queues at the first tee at weekends, especially.

Formosa Auckland Country Club

Jack Lachlan Dr, Beachlands, Ph: 536 5895.

Website: www.formosa.co.nz

Open: 7 days 7 am–dusk. Bookings essential.

Fees: $65 New Zealand affiliated, $125 non-affiliated, $55 members & their guests (all include use of facilities), facilities (locker room, spa, sauna). Hire: clubs $35, carts $30, shoes $10. Summer specials will apply.

New Zealand's longest (6650 m off pro-tees) and most spacious golf course, with sea views of the nearby Hauraki

Gulf from 15 of the 18 holes. Designed by New Zealand's most experienced professional golfer Bob Charles, and the venue for the 1998 New Zealand Open. Wind gusts from the ocean can make it a challenging course. Striking palm and water-feature layout. Restaurant open 7 days, from 7 am breakfast to late dinner.

Gulf Harbour Country
Gulf Harbour Dr, Gulf Harbour, Ph: 09 428 1380. (Golf Shop)
Website: www.gulf-harbour.co.nz
Open: 7 days, 7 am–dusk. Soft spikes only.
Fees: Mon to Sun, $95 New Zealand and Australian affiliated, non-affiliated $110 for 18 holes, includes golf cart hire. Bookings essential. Hire: clubs $30 (regular), $50 (executive).

Purpose-built course across rolling hills with spectacular views. Attached to plush yachting marina and European village-like architecture. Leading European golfer Colin Montgomerie has praised the course.

Howick Golf Club
32 Musick Point Rd, Bucklands Beach, Ph: 535 1001.
Pro-Shop open 7 days. Bookings advised, Ph: 535 1004.
Fees: 7 days, non-affiliated green fees $40, affiliated green fees $30, Sunday after 12.30 pm green fee players allowed. Hire: $15 (half set), carts available, members $25, non-members $30, trundlers $4. Tuition: $40 (30 mins), $75 (1hr).

Maungakiekie Golf Club
5 Anita Ave, Mt Roskill, Ph: 621 0090.
Website: www.maungakiekie.nzgolf.net
Open Sun to Fri, dawn to dusk. Sat, members only.
Fees: Non-affiliated M/F $50, Sat & Sun $60, (New Zealand affiliated M/F $30, Sat & Sun $40). Bookings essential. Hire: clubs $30, carts $30, trundlers $5. Tuition: on request.

Attractive, undulating course with extensive tree-lined fairways and spectacular views of the Waitakere Ranges.

Papakura Camp Golf Club

Walters Rd, Papakura. Ph: 298 3858.

Open: 7 days, 7 am–dusk.

Fees: $25 affiliated, $15 with a member. Bookings advised. Hire: clubs $5 (limited selection, trundler free), carts $20.

Relaxed, easy-walking course with very well-drained fairways in park-like setting.

Peninsula Golf Club

Main Highway, Orewa, Ph: 09 426 4001.

Website: www.peninsulagolf.co.nz

Open: 7 days, summer 7.30 am–dusk, winter 8 am–dusk; Sat members only.

Fees: $30 affiliated $40 non-affiliated. Hire: clubs $30 (with trundler), carts $25. Tuition: $40 per 30 mins. Bookings essential, pro-shop, Ph: 09 426 5776.

Fairly gentle course with extensive sea views over the Hauraki Gulf, on the doorstep of the America's Cup course.

Pupuke Golf Club

231 East Coast Rd, Campbells Bay, Ph: 410 7906.

Website: www.nzgolfcourses.co.nz/pupuke

Open: 7 days, daylight–dusk.

Fees: $40 affiliated, $50 non-affiliated, $35 member's guests. Hire: clubs $20, trundlers $5, carts $25. Tuition: $40 per 30 mins. Bookings essential, pro-shop, Ph: 410 3045.

Full bar and catering facilities available 7 days a week. Undulating, tree-lined course makes for a challenging round of golf with spectacular views of the sea. One minute from Campbells Bay beach.

Takapuna Golf Course & Driving Range

Thomas Park, 27 Northcote Rd, Takapuna, Ph: 443 5002.

Open: 7 days, daylight–dusk.

Website: www.takapunagolf.co.nz

Fees: $22 weekdays, $25 weekends (+ Pub Hols). Hire: clubs $16 (half set) $28 (full set), Junior half sets $10; carts $30, trundlers $4. Bookings advised. TaylorMade Rentals available. Tuition: $45 per 30 mins.

Easy-walking course with tree-lined fairways, 5 mins from downtown Takapuna and bordering Northern Motorway.

Titirangi Golf Club

Links Rd, New Lynn, Ph: 827 5749.

Website: www.titirangigolf.co.nz

Open: 7 days, daylight–dusk (Sat, members only).

Fees: $60 affiliated, $40 member's guest. Non-affiliated and overseas visitors $120. Bookings essential, Ph: 827 3967. Tuition: $35 per 30 mins.

Alister MacKenzie-designed, undulating course providing an interesting and challenging round of golf. Scenic setting, surrounded by native bush.

Wattle Downs Golf and Country Club

Wattle Farm Rd Extension, Manurewa, Ph: 268 1929.

Open: 7 days, 8 am–8 pm.

Fees: $20 (9 holes), $25 (18 holes). Juniors (under 18) $5 (9 or 18 holes). Bookings essential Sat & Sun. Hire: clubs $5 for 9 holes, $10 for 18 holes, trundlers $4, carts $20.

Flat, easy-to-walk course with tight tree-lined fairways.

DRIVING RANGES

A bucket of balls costs from as little as $5 with clubs also available for a small hire fee. Most of the following ranges are open 7 days, and bookings are recommended:

Aviation Country Club, Tom Pearce Dr, Auckland Airport, Ph: 275 6265.

Golf Today, Ellerslie Racecourse, Greenlane Rd (near Ascot Hospital), Greenlane, Ph: 522 2124.

Golf Today, 69–71 Ballarat St, Ellerslie, Ph: 526 0056.

Big Swing Golf New Zealand, 79 Ormiston Rd, East Tamaki, Ph: 274 4479. Website: www.bigswing.co.nz

Premiere International Driving Range, Fred Thomas Dr, Takapuna, Ph: 489 5374.

Takapuna Golf Course & Driving Range, Thomas Park, 27 Northcote Rd, Takapuna, Ph: 443 5002.

TENNIS

Anyone for tennis? If you're not watching the game, grab a racquet and head down to any of the several courts you can hire around Auckland. Some of them will have a racquet and balls available for hire also. Bookings essential.

Auckland Tennis Inc
ASB Tennis Centre, 72 Stanley St, Parnell, Ph: 373 3623.
Website: www.aucklandtennis.co.nz
Seven outdoor courts, five indoor courts. Open 7 days, 7 am–10 pm. Court bookings advised.

Vodafone Tennis Park
69 Merton Rd, Glen Innes, Ph: 528 9782.
Website: www.aucklandtennis.co.nz
Court bookings advised. 15 outdoor courts, 6 indoor courts.
Open: Mon to Fri 7 am–10 pm, Sat & Sun 8 am–10 pm.

Bartercard Manukau Tennis Centre
Sports Bowl, Te Irirangi Dr, Manukau, Ph: 274 4577.
Court bookings advised. Four astro-grass courts and four sealed courts.
Open: Mon to Fri 9 am–8.30 pm, summer weekends 8 am–6 pm, winter weekends 10 am–6 pm.

Windmill Rd Tennis Courts
48 Windmill Rd, Mt Eden, Ph: 630 3061.
10 outdoor courts. No bookings taken. Casual 'roll up and play'.
Open: Mon to Sun 7 am–9 pm.

TENPIN BOWLING

Strike. Spare. Learning the language at the tenpin bowling centres is as much fun as rattling the pins onto the floor at the end of the bowling lanes. Note: wearing the special shoes, on hire at each venue, is compulsory. Bowling balls come in various weights and have different finger-hole sizes to suit the carrying capacity of all. Free for spectators.

Panmure Superbowl, 525 Ellerslie Panmure Highway, Ph: 570 9130.

Superstrike Tenpin Bowling Centre, 573 Great South Rd, Manukau City, Ph: 277 9296.

Tenpin Takapuna, 3 Fred Thomas Dr, Takapuna, Ph: 0800 836 746.

Tenpin Westgate, Westgate Shopping Centre, Hobsonville Rd (end of Northwestern Motorway), Massey, Ph: 831 0260.

Tenpin Lincoln Road, 199 Lincoln Rd, Henderson, Ph: 0800 836 746.

ICE SKATING

Get yourself out on that ice, even in Auckland's summer weather (especially then). Slide around the ice upright or otherwise. Admire the skill of the kids. Great fun in short bursts if you're a novice. Avoid the flash Torvill and Dean skaters pirouetting past, but admire from a distance.

Paradise Ice Rink
136 Lansford Cres, Avondale, Ph: 828 8286.
490 Ti Rakau Dr, Botany Downs, Ph: 273 2999.

Water World

Auckland has plenty of beaches, but for those who prefer inland conditions the swimming pools around the city offer plenty of variety. And safe for the children too.

FREE COMMUNITY POOLS

Manurewa Leisure Centre
Francis St, Manurewa, Ph: 267 7072.
Open: Mon to Fri 6 am–5.45 pm (swim club/sauna/sunbeds); Sat, Sun & public holidays 9 am–4.45 pm.

Norman Kirk Memorial Pool
Newberry St, Otara, Ph: 274 6917.
Open: Mon to Fri 6 am–6 pm; Sat & Sun 8 am–6 pm.

Papatoetoe Centennial Swimming Pool
Sutton Cres, Paptoetoe, Ph: 278 4167.
Open: Mon to Fri 6 am–6.45 pm; Sat, Sun & public holidays 9 am–6.45 pm.

Totara Park Pool
Wairere Rd, Manurewa, Ph: 267 7497.
Open: Nov to Mar.

POOLS WITH ENTRY FEE

Birkenhead Leisure Centre
Mahara Ave, Birkenhead, Ph: 418 4109.
Open: 7 days, Nov to Apr 12 pm–6 pm. Closed Christmas day. Entry fees: adults $3, children $2.50, concession cards available.

Glenfield Leisure Centre
Bentley Ave, Glenfield, Ph: 444 6340.

Open: Mon to Fri 5.30 am–9 pm; Sat & Sun 8 am–6 pm; public holidays
9 am–5 pm. Closed Christmas day. Entry fees: adults $5, children $3,
concession cards available.

Mt Eden Swimming Pool

30A Bellevue Rd, Mt Eden, Ph: 630 1123.

Open: Mon to Fri 6 am–9 pm; Sat & Sun 8 am–7 pm. Entry fees: adults $4 ($5
swim, sauna and steam room), children $3 ($4 swim, sauna and steam room),
family (2 adults & 2 children) $10 ($14 swim, sauna and steam room).

Olympic Pools and Fitness Centre

Broadway, Newmarket, Ph: 522 4414.

Website: www.olympicpools.co.nz

Open: Mon to Fri 5.45 am–10 pm; Sat, Sun & public holidays 7 am–8 pm. Entry
fees: adults $5, children/senior citizens $3.

Onehunga Aquasports

Jellicoe Park (off Quadrant St), Park Gardens Rd, Onehunga, Ph: 636 5330.

Open: Mon to Fri 5.15 am–9 pm; Sat, Sun & public holidays 7 am–7 pm. Closed
Christmas day & New Year's day. Entry fees: adults $4, children $2, family
(2 adults & 3 children) $10.

Philips Aquatic Centre

38 Alberton Ave, Mt Albert, Ph: 815 7005, Infoline Ph: 815 7001.

Open: Mon to Thurs 6 am–8 pm; Fri 6 am–9 pm; Sat, Sun & public holidays
7 am–9 pm. Closed Christmas day. Entry fees: adults $7, children/senior
citizens $5, children under 5 & non-swimmers $2, family (2 adults &
2 children, or 1 adult & 3 children) $20.

Roskill Aquasport (Cameron Pool)

53 Arundel St, Mt Roskill, Ph: 625 8751.

Open: Mon to Thurs 6 am–9 pm; Fri 6 am–8 pm; Sat 7 am–6 pm;
Sun 8.30 am–6 pm. Closed Christmas day & Good Friday. Entry fees: adults $4,
children $2, family (2 adults & 2 children) $10.

Takapuna Aquatic Centre

Killarney St, Takapuna, Ph: 486 3286.

Open: Mon, Wed, Fri 6 am–8.30 pm; Tues, Thurs, 6 am–6 pm; Sat, Sun & public
holidays, 10 am–6 pm. Closed Christmas day. Entry fees: adults $5,
children $3, family (2 adults & 3 children) $15.

Waitakere City Aquatic Centre

20 Alderman Dr, Henderson, Ph: 836 8066.

Open: 7 days, 5.45 am–9.30 pm. Entry fees (includes use of spa, sauna & steam room): adults $5 ($4 Mon to Fri 9 am–2 pm); children $3.50; family (2 adults & up to 4 children) $20.

Waiwera Thermal Resort

State Highway 1,7 Waiwera Rd, Waiwera, Infoline Ph: 09 302 1684.

Freephone: 0800 WAIWERA (0800 924 937).

Website: www.waiwera.co.nz

Open: 7 days, 9 am–10 pm. Entry fees (includes use of pools & waterslides): adults $18, senior citizens $8, children (5–14 yrs) $10 (4 yrs & under $5); family (2 adults & 2 children) $47; concessions available. Fees include Hibiscus movie pool: 5 films screen from 11.20 am (9 am during school holidays) to 8 pm.

YMCA Glen Innes Fitness and Aquatic Centre

122 Elstree Ave, Glen Innes, Ph: 527 3260.

Open: Mon to Fri 5.30 am–9 pm; Sat, Sun & public holidays, 7.30 am–7 pm. Closed Christmas day. Entry fees: adults $3.50 ($5.50 includes spa & steam room), children $2 ($3 spa & steam room). No family concession.

YMCA Point Erin Pools

Shelly Beach Rd, Herne Bay, Ph: 376 6863.

Open: Mon to Fri 6.30 am–8 pm; Sat, Sun & public holidays, 9 am–8 pm through summer (Nov to Apr). Entry fees: adults $4; students $3.50; children (under 12 yrs) $3 (under 5 yrs) $2; concessions available.

YMCA Tepid Baths

100 Customs St West, Auckland Central, Ph: 379 4745.

Open: Mon to Fri 6 am–9 pm; Sat, Sun & public holidays, 7 am–7 pm. Entry fees: adults $4.50; students $3.50; children (under 12 yrs) $2; senior citizens $2; concessions available.

DIVE CENTRES

NZ Underwater Association

1/40 Mt Eden Rd, Mt Eden, Ph: 623 3252.

Website: www.nzunderwater.org.nz

Non-profit organisation representing the diving industry. A useful contact to put you in touch with suitable diving courses.

Walks Galore

Avoid the traffic problems, take a walk. Strolling through parts of Auckland city or in one of the many parks or urban nature trails, you get a more relaxed perspective on Auckland. For details on all these walks, get a pamphlet and map from any visitors centre, the Department of Conservation office in the Ferry Buildings, the Auckland City Council or the Auckland Regional Council.

COAST-TO-COAST

The major walk across town is the Coast-to-Coast from the waterfront in downtown Auckland to the waterfront at Onehunga on the Manukau harbour. It is about 16 km (four hours' walk) one way, and takes in Albert Park and Auckland University, Auckland Domain, Mt Eden Domain and One Tree Hill/Cornwall Park Domain before the downhill leg to Onehunga. Then catch a bus or taxi back.

HISTORIC PARNELL

Parnell is Auckland's oldest suburb, established by the mechanics and tradesmen who settled at Mechanics Bay on the foreshore, and by landed gentry (Judge's Bay was named for the first chief justice Sir William Martin). A Maori pa (fortified village) was located on Resolution Pt above the present site of the Parnell baths. This walk encompasses elegantly restored villas, historic churches, a short section of bush, and fine restaurants, galleries and design shops.

OLD DEVONPORT

This one-hour walk begins in the King Edward Reserve just near the ferry wharf. Scattered along the whole route are early colonial buildings, with columned verandahs and wooden fretwork. At the flagstaff in the reserve, members of the British navy came ashore in 1840 to establish European settlement. Maori colonisation is recorded in the memorial to the arrival of the Tainui canoe. An optional walk up Mt Victoria will be rewarded with stunning views of the city and its surrounds. There are numerous cafes for refreshments.

ONEHUNGA HERITAGE WALKS

The word 'onehunga' means 'landing place' and the suburb is rich in Maori and European history. In Jellicoe Park at the corner of Quadrant Road and Grey Street, there are three museums, an 1860s defence blockhouse, Journey's End, the replica of an 1850 double-unit 'fencible' cottage for the defence forces, and Laishley house, built in 1859 as a manse for the Congregational Church. A number of other historic buildings line the walk, including the old Carnegie Free Library building, now a restaurant.

TAHUNA-TOREA NATURE RESERVE

This 25 ha wilderness of mangrove lagoon, swampland and coast on the Tamaki Estuary (access from Vista Crescent or West Tamaki Road car park, Glen Innes) is home to myriad birds. The name 'Tahuna-Torea' means 'gathering place of the oystercatcher' and is taken from the name of a 1.5-km sandspit beach. Historically, Tahuna-Torea was an excellent site for shellfish, fish and birds for the tangata whenua (people of the land), the local tribe Ngati Paoa. The 45-minute walk offers the opportunity to view a wide range of birdlife. Wear suitable footwear for possibly muddy tracks.

EASY WALKS IN THE WAITAKERES

There are more than 40 walking tracks through the bush in the vicinity of the Piha and Karekare beaches. A sample, using information from the Arataki Visitors Centre (6 km from Titirangi along the Scenic Dr, Waitakere Ranges):

PIHA

Tasman Lookout Track

Watch mesmerised as the full force of the Tasman Sea surges through The Gap beside the Tasman Lookout Track. The track (40 minutes return) at the southern end of Piha climbs steeply at first, then levels for a view of The Gap and Taitomo Island.

Kitekite Falls

From the end of Glen Esk Rd, follow this popular, well-formed streamside track to the Kitekite Falls with its swimming hole (one hour return walk).

Byers Walk

From the end of Glen Esk Rd, an easy path following the Glen Esk Stream through groves of ponga and nikau forest (30 minutes return walk).

KAREKARE

Pohutukawa Glade Walk

Track leads from picnic area to the south end of this powerful surf beach where scenes from Jane Campion's Cannes award-winning film *The Piano* were shot. The walk can be extended further along the beach and back beside Karekare stream.

Karekare Falls

A 10-minute walk up the Lone Kauri Road from the beach car park and along the Taraire Track. The first part of the track leads to the base of the falls and the picnic area, once the site of the Karekare sawmill.

Mercer Bay loop

From the end of the Te Ahuahu Road (off the Piha Road, 4 km before Piha) the track takes you to the edge of the ocean for spectacular views along the coast (one hour return walk).

Bethells Beach (Te Henga)

Lake Wainamu Track. (From Bethells Road, 2 km before Te Henga or Bethells Beach). Follow a shallow, meandering stream through wind-sculpted sand dunes to reach this hidden lake (one hour return walk).

Cascade Falls

Walk to the Cascade Falls and view bush and forest as it was in New Zealand's early days, with a delightfully hidden vista of the Cascade waterfall at the end.

KAURI WALKS

One of the great clean-green secrets in Auckland is the number of kauri bush walks in the heart of suburban North Shore. Marvel at the 300-year-old kauri trees standing just metres from busy roads. Listen for tui sounds and look out for a tranquil creek in the heart of dense bush, just 15 minutes from where you left the car in the middle of a housing estate. Wonder at the cathedral-like grove of giant puriri trees next to the Takapuna Cricket Club grounds. Listen to the silence in the heart of Le Roy's bush, just a short walk from a busy main road. 'You would never know you were in the city', marvelled one visitor. Deep bush, easy walking tracks, peace in the city – you have to see it to believe it.

Kauri Point Centennial Park
Onetaunga Rd, Birkenhead.

Extensive bush area. Well-formed, well-signposted up-and-down walking tracks (some steps). More pine, ponga and manuka than kauri. Harbour views.

Chatswood Reserve
Portsea Pl, Birkenhead.

Meandering bush reserve in the middle of a mix-and-match suburb. Good tracks, cute creek with solid wooden bridges. Infant kauris galore plus some excellent teenage specimens down the track from the entrance, 300–400 years old. Remember, unless you exit by the same path that you entered, you may end up streets away from where you parked the car.

Le Roy's Bush
12 Le Roy Tce/ 32 Hinemoa St/ 210 Onewa Rd, Birkenhead.

Well-maintained paths. From the Le Roy Terrace entrance, note the tree root arching over the path. Tuis and wood pigeons sound more clearly while suburban noise recedes with each step into the depths.

Kauri Glen
Kauri Glen Rd (off Onewa Rd), Northcote.

Entrance beside Northcote College. Alternating pockets of dense bush and sunlit kauri groves on the ridges. Keep to the stepped paths.

Eskdale Reserve
84 Eskdale Rd, Birkenhead.

Easy walking track. Scrubby bush at first, and it takes a while to escape sounds of surrounding suburbia. Long track leads to Birkenhead Domain (map of tracks is beside Eskdale Rd entrance). Biggest trees here are kanuka and pine. Not jogger-free.

Kauri Park
Rangitira Rd, Birkenhead.

Great notable 300-year-old kauris just metres down the well-presented track from Rangatira Rd entrance (100 metres down on left from caravan park), Birkenhead. Loop path runs

beside the big trees, but you can spot other great trunks through the bush. A taste of what New Zealand must have looked like 100 years and more ago, and a small miracle of preservation.

Smith's Bush

Flat, small bush area boasting magnificent giant puriri trees, with attendant epiphytes in full view. Enter beside the Takapuna Cricket Club clubhouse or netball courts off Onewa Domain (opposite the Poenamo pub). Watch for tree roots studding the path throughout this spacious patch of bush, passed indifferently by high-speed traffic on the adjacent motorway.

Foreign Consulates

Foreign Representatives & Organisations in
Auckland

AUSTRALIA

Consul, Level 7, 188 Quay St, Auckland Central, Ph: 921 8800.

AUSTRIA

Consul, 98 Kitchener Rd, Milford, Ph: 489 8249.

Austrian Club, PO 31330, Milford, Ph: 418 2871 or 625 4650.

BANGLADESH

Bangladesh NZ Friendship Society, Contact: Ataur Rahman, Ph: 410 2335.

BELGIUM

Consul, Level 2, Orica House, Cnr Carlton Gore Rd & Kingdon St, Newmarket,
Ph: 915 9150.

CAMBODIA

Auckland Cambodian Chinese Kung Luc, 55 Sikkim Cres, Manukau, Auckland,
Ph: 263 4991 (2001).

Auckland Khmer Buddhist Association Inc, 7 Yates Road, Mangere, Auckland,
Ph: 275 5685.

CANADA

Consul, 48 Emily Place, Auckland, Ph: 309 3690, Fax: 307 3111.

CHILE

Hon Consul, G J P Williams, Ph: 373 4602.

CHINA

Consul, 588 Great South Rd, Greenlane, Ph: 525 1589.

China-New Zealand Associations Inc, Contact: Stephen Wong, Ph: 274 9801, Mob: 027 478 5819.

Auckland Chinese Community Centres, 1 New North Rd, Eden Tce, Auckland, Ph: 309 3033; and 99 Taylor Rd, Mangere Bridge, Auckland, Ph: 634 5671.

COOK ISLANDS

Consul, 1/127 Symonds St, Auckland Central, Ph: 366 1100.

Cook Islands Charitable Trust, Ph: 256 1403.

CROATIA

Consul, 291 Lincoln Rd, Henderson, Ph: 836 5581, Fax: 836 5481.

Croatian Centre, 161 MacLeod Rd, Henderson, Auckland, Ph: 836 6550.

DENMARK

Consul, P O Box 619, Ph: 537 3099.

The Danish Society Inc, 6 Rockridge Ave, Penrose, Auckland, Ph: 580 3103.

FRANCE

Consul, Level 2, 63 Albert Street, Auckland Central, Ph: 379 5850.

Alliance Française d'Auckland Inc, 9 Kirk Street, Grey Lynn, Auckland, Ph: 376 0009, Fax: 376 0098, PO Box 78329.

FINLAND

Hon Consul, Mr Ari Hallenberg, Prime Time Communications Ltd, 10 Heather St, Parnell, Auckland, Ph: 309 2969 or 358 4915, Fax: 357 0466, PO Box 8553, Symonds St.

GERMANY

Hon Consul, 52 Symonds St, Auckland Central, Ph: 913 3674.
German Society, Ph: 274 5447.
Goethe Society, Auckland University German Department, Ph: 373 7599.
German Translations, PO Box 32385, Devonport, Auckland, Ph: 445 8807.

GREECE

Greek Community of Auckland Inc, PO Box 10 220, Dominion Road, Auckland,
Ph: 638 6146.

HUNGARY

Consul, Level 1, 334 Ponsonby Rd, PO Box 47824, Ponsonby, Ph: 376 6155.
Auckland Hungarian Club, Ph: 523 3855.

INDIA

Auckland Indian Association, 145 New North Rd, Eden Terrace, Auckland,
Ph: 357 0665.

New Zealand Sikh Society, Auckland Branch Inc, Cnr Princes & Albert Sts,
Otahuhu, Auckland, Ph: 276 9043, Fax: 276 9236.

IRAN

Iranian Community Trust, 4b Olympic Pl, New Lynn, Auckland, Ph: 826 3940.

IRELAND

Consul, Level 6, 18 Shortland St, Auckland Central, Ph: 977 2252, Fax: 977 2256.
Auckland Irish Society, 29 Great North Rd, Grey Lynn, Auckland, Ph: 378 6897.

ISRAEL

Israel Information Office, PO Box 4315, Auckland, Ph: 309 9444, Fax: 373 2283.

ITALY

Consular Agency, 102 Kitchener Rd, Milford, Auckland, Ph: 489 9632.

JAPAN

Consul, Level 12, ASB Bank Centre, 135 Albert St, Auckland Central,
Ph: 303 4106, Fax. 377 7784.
Japanese Society of Auckland, Ph: 366 4408.

KIRIBATI

Hon Consul Raymond D Mann, 3 Gladstone Rd, Northcote, Ph: 419 0404,
Fax: 419 1414, PO Box 40205, Glenfield.

KOREA

Consul, Level 10 Toshiba House, 396 Queen St, Auckland Central, Ph: 379 0818.
Korean Society of NZ, PO Box 8598, Symonds St, Ph: 309 6001 or 309 6605.

MALAYSIA

Consul, 19 Morgan St, Newmarket, Ph: 355 6016.

MALTA

Consul, Ph: 027 291 2059.

MYANMAR (BURMA)

Auckland Myanmar Buddhist Association Trust, 3075A Great North Rd,
New Lynn, Ph: 826 3490.

NEPAL

New Zealand Nepal Society Inc, 8 Ratanui St, Henderson, Ph: 837 7995.

NORWAY

Consul, 11 Ranleigh Rd, Mt Albert, PO Box 2364, Shortland St, Ph: 355 1830.

THE NETHERLANDS

Consul First Floor, 57 Symonds Street, Auckland, Ph: 379 5399.

Friendly Support Network of The Netherlands Community, 6 Hamurata Pl,
Te Atatu, Auckland, Ph: 834 6247.

PERU

Consul, 199–209 Great North Rd, Grey Lynn, Auckland, Ph: 376 9400.

PHILIPPINES

Consul, First Floor, 121 Beach Rd, Auckland Central, Ph: 303 2423.

Council of Auckland Philippine Organisations (CAPO) Inc, PO Box 33-1235,
Takapuna, Ph: 529 1641.

POLAND

Hon Consul, John Roy, 51 Grange Rd, Howick, Ph: 533-5166.

Auckland Polish Association, Ph: 849 2836.

RUSSIA

Russian Info-Line, PO Box 25827, St Heliers, Ph: 528 3524.

Russian Society of New Zealand, Villa Dalmicija, 10–14 New North Rd, Eden Tce, Ph: 303 3020.

New Zealand–Russia & Sovereign States Association Ltd, 3B Dallinghoe Cres, Milford, Ph: 410 7568.

SOMALIA

Auckland Somali Community Association Inc, Graeme Breed Dr, Three Kings, Ph: 624 6051.

SOUTH AFRICA

Afrikaans Klub, P O Box 300674, Albany, Ph: 478 2291.

South Africa New Zealand Charitable Trust Inc (SANZ), 2 Northcroft St, Takapuna, Ph: 486 4442.

SPAIN & LATIN AMERICA

Spanish & Latin American Services, P O Box 8727, Symonds St, Ph: 627 5917.

Auckland Latin American Community, PO Box 13741, Onehunga, Ph: 636 8776. (see also Chile and Peru)

SRI LANKA

New Zealand Sri Lanka Buddhist Trust, 11 Pukeora Road, Otahuhu, Ph: 270 2898.

SWEDEN

Consul, 13TH Floor, Simpson Grierson Building, 92-96 Albert St, Auckland Central, Ph: 373 5332.

Swedish Association, Contact: Ingela Johannisson, Ph: 368 4740 or 443 7602.

TAIWAN

Economic and Cultural Office, Level 18 Westpac Trust Tower, 120 Albert St, Auckland Central, PO Box 4018, Ph: 303 3903, Fax: 302 3399.

THAILAND

Consul, Level 5, 18 Shortland St, Auckland Central, Ph: 373 3166.

TIBET

Tibetan Community, Ph: 483 6066 or 483 7275.

TONGA

Tongan Tamaki Langafonua Community Centre Inc, 183 Taniwha Road, Glen Innes, Ph: 528 8280; and 141 Taniwha Street, Glen Innes, Ph: 528 8261.

TURKEY

New Zealand Turkish Intercultural Society, 399 Khyber Pass Road, Newmarket, Ph: 524 2437.

TUVALU

Consul, PO Box 100375, North Shore Mail Centre, Ph: 410 6463.

Auckland Tuvaluan Society Inc, 365 Great North Rd, Henderson, Ph: 836 3635.

UNITED KINGDOM

British Consul, 17TH Floor NZI House, 151 Queen St, Auckland, Ph: 303 2973 (trade and investment).

British Council, 17TH Floor NZI House, 151 Queen Street, Auckland, Ph: 373 4545, Fax: 373 4479.

UNITED STATES OF AMERICA

Consul, Level 3, Citibank Centre, 23 Customs St, Auckland Central, Ph: 303 2724.

WALES

Auckland Welsh Club, PO Box 11455, Ellerslie, Ph: 524 7767.

WESTERN SAMOA

Consul, 283 Karangahape Rd, Newton, Ph: 303 1012, after hours Ph: 524 7643.

Accommodation

Your stay in a city can often be made or spoiled by the accommodation you choose.

Auckland – with more space and a smaller population than most major cities overseas – has an enormous variety of places to stay. There have never been more beds available in Auckland, with the America's Cup and ever-increasing tourist numbers causing visitors to pour into the city. While a lot of these are upmarket, central-city hotels for travellers with deep pockets, the buoyant market has resulted in enterprising families with characterful homes and rooms to spare opening up bed-and-breakfasts all over the place; and Auckland will never be short of motels.

So, take your pick. You can rest your head cheaply at a backpackers or motor camp, choose a motel that suits your budget and the energy levels of your children, do the intimate weekend thing at a bed-and-breakfast or blow the week's grocery money at a fancy city hotel.

All the usual hotel and motel chains are listed in the Auckland Yellow Pages (website: www.yellowpages.co.nz) along with those great little B&Bs and motor camps. Call into any inner-city bookshop to pick up a copy of the AA or Jason's accommodation guides for detailed listings of all

types of accommodation. Check with the local tourist visitor centres (Tourism Auckland, Amex Viaduct Harbour, cnr Quay and Hobson Sts, Auckland, Ph: 979 2333; Sky City Atrium, cnr Federal and Victoria Sts, Auckland Central, Ph: 363 6000). Alternatively, if you have access to the Internet, some useful websites with information about accommodation in Auckland include:

www.aatourism.co.nz

www.jasons.co.nz

www.aucklandnz.com

It's also always worth checking for good deals on www.wotif.com which features last-minute online booking options at hugely discounted rates.

For the more budget-conscious, try the Youth Hostel Association, Ph: 0800 278 299, or the YMCA, Ph: 303 2068.